MW01274354

Dwight F. Burlingame, Timothy L. Seiler,
Eugene R. Tempel
Indiana University Center on Philanthropy
EDITORS

SMALL NONPROFITS

STRATEGIES FOR FUNDRAISING SUCCESS

Mary Louise Mussoline
MLM Associates

EDITOR

NUMBER 20, SUMMER 1998

SMALL NONPROFITS: STRATEGIES FOR FUNDRAISING SUCCESS
Mary Louise Mussoline (ed.)
New Directions for Philanthropic Fundraising, No. 20, Summer 1998
Dwight F. Burlingame, Timothy L. Seiler, Eugene R. Tempel, Editors

NEW DIRECTIONS FOR PHILANTHROPIC FUNDRAISING is indexed in Higher Education
Abstracts and Philanthropic Index.

Microfilm copies of issues and articles are available in 16 mm and 35 mm, as well as
microfiche in 105 mm, through University Microfilms Inc., 300 North Zeeb Road,
Ann Arbor, Michigan 48106-1346.

ISSN 1072-172X   ISBN 0-7879-4270-7

NEW DIRECTIONS FOR PHILANTHROPIC FUNDRAISING is part of The Jossey-Bass
Nonprofit Sector Series and is published quarterly by Jossey-Bass Inc., Publishers,
350 Sansome Street, San Francisco, California 94104-1342.

SUBSCRIPTIONS cost $67.00 for individuals and $115.00 for institutions, agencies,
and libraries. Prices subject to change. Refer to the Ordering Information page
at the back of this issue.

EDITORIAL CORRESPONDENCE should be sent to the editor, Dwight F. Burlingame,
Center on Philanthropy, Indiana University, 550 West North Street, Suite 301,
Indianapolis, IN 46202-3162.

www.josseybass.com

Printed in the United States of America on acid-free recycled paper containing 100
percent recovered waste paper, of which at least 20 percent is postconsumer waste.

Contents

they serve. This chapter explains how organizations can strengthen their funding base by bringing all constituencies—based on gender, race, age, and so on—into fundraising.

Editor's Notes

THROUGH THEIR WORK to provide service to people in need, small nonprofits are the heart and soul of the independent sector in this country. As advocates for the poor, builders of community, and guardians of the environment, small organizations are big players in the work of the not-for-profit world.

Excluding most religious congregations, there are approximately 546,000 nonprofit organizations in the United States. Of that number, 70 percent are organizations with budgets less than $25,000 and another 12 percent have budgets under $100,000. These organizations reflect the significant dedication of people to their missions and their communities. Millions of people serve in a staffing capacity or as volunteer leaders in these organizations. Add to those the people involved as recipients of service or "customers" to get a true picture of the vast impact of small nonprofits on the quality of life for so many citizens.

Small organizations differ from their large counterparts in many ways beyond size of staff and budget. Generally, they come into existence because their issue is just emerging and is not yet addressed by other organizations or because the needs of a specific population are not being adequately met by others. For example, in the 1970s, the women's movement brought the issue of domestic violence into public view. Women in communities throughout the country established a network of "safe homes" to provide emergency shelter to women fleeing abusive relationships. This grassroots movement then spawned thousands of independent shelters to provide a longer stay and services to help battered women leave abusive relationships and establish new lives for themselves and their children. As understanding grew regarding the issues involved, other approaches were formed. Counseling programs for men who batter, legal advocacy for women, protective legislation, and public education are examples. Many volunteers became involved on various levels such as staffing hotlines, providing overnight shelter coverage, sponsoring legislation, hosting fundraising events, and drafting bylaws to establish these new nonprofit organizations. Dedicated people provided much needed assistance to their neighbors and also transformed the country's thinking about issues that in the past had been a private, deadly family matter.

Today, many of these organizations continue to exist in a much more established way, receiving funding from local, state, and federal governments, as well as from United Way. This was unheard of in the early stages of the movement. The hundreds of organizations that were established in response to the AIDS epidemic are a more recent example of this type of community organizing.

Even as these organizations mature and grow in size and scope, they continue to operate with passion and commitment because of their strong mission-driven focus.

This volume is written with both the strengths and weaknesses of small organizations in mind. The authors consider areas of special importance for small organizations: diversity of income sources, strength of the board of directors, involvement of diverse constituencies in fundraising—issues that all small nonprofits face today. They also discuss more focused topics important to small organizations, such as the conversion of special events donors to annual fund donors and the important human aspects of working with volunteers.

Although securing financial resources is the central theme of this volume, it is clear that strength of mission and leadership are inseparable from all discussion of fundraising. A relevant mission and strong, dedicated leaders are requirements for successful fundraising for all organizations, and they are even more important for the smaller ones.

The long-term viability of small organizations is directly related to their ability to raise private funds and maintain donors. It is critical to have a diverse fundraising program that reaches all donor markets. It is wise to seek small and large gifts from individuals and grants from businesses, foundations, religious institutions, and associations. It is essential to develop a strategy to reach all those markets, while adequately using available human resources and skills within the organization. This is clearly a challenge for small organizations. In Chapter One, Patricia Wyzbinski, Pam Moore, and Scott Gelzer provide a step-by-step method for analyzing current fundraising strengths and the fundraising environment and for developing a strategic plan for securing income. This process encourages high volunteer involvement in analysis and planning—a practice that will ultimately increase volunteer ownership in fundraising, resulting in a high-quality annual fund.

The ability of small organizations to carry out their vision depends on the strength of their foundations. The board of directors carries the mission of the organization into the community and brings the views of the community into the organization. Its importance to the health of an organization and its financial base is primary. In a small organization, the board members do work that would be undertaken by staff in a large organization. Most small organizations report difficulty in creating and operating good working boards. In Chapter Two, Frank Martinelli provides a primer on the value of taking the time to establish a solid board of directors and suggests ways to ensure that this body is properly leading the organization.

Getting and keeping quality staff is very important to small organizations. At issue too is preventing burnout. Without a doubt, staff in these organizations serve in multiple roles: administration, program, fundraising, human resources, and community relations are just a few. Large organizations have three or four people assigned to tasks that may be the responsibility of one staff person in a small organization. In Chapter Three, Marissa Weaver discusses methods to involve volunteers paid through public programs to serve as staff members for a one-person or small staff operation. Weaver also suggests ways to accomplish staff functions and involve board members in important fundraising efforts in the one-person shop.

Although academicians and administrators discuss the role of volunteers in the nonprofit sector, it helps to hear from those who actually do the work. In Chapter Four, Barbara A. Stein, a community activist and philanthropist who puts her work where her money is, provides valuable lessons that come from working with volunteers. This account of some great and not-so-great moments working with staff and other volunteers over a forty-year volunteer career reminds us that volunteers have a lot of choices when it comes to where they will devote their energies. People who volunteer have full lives outside of their work for nonprofits. We compete with responsibilities to family, friends, work and educational pursuits, spiritual needs, and recreational activities. It is wise to make the best use of the time people devote to helping their community through their work with nonprofits.

There is much discussion these days about diversity and increasing diversity within organizations, yet the concept is one of the most misunderstood in the nonprofit world. To many, it means adding people of color to an organization's board or staff. But when considering diversity we must look at gender, age, sexual orientation, economic ability, ethnic and racial background, and so on. We each have our own misconceptions about other people and need to continue to remind ourselves that we all can be successful in fundraising. The more diverse our solicitors, the more diverse our funding base will be. In Chapter Five, Kim Klein has written a thought-provoking piece that challenges us to bring all our constituencies into fundraising and reap the benefits.

Whenever I tell people that my profession is fundraising, I am always asked immediately about fundraising events. The fact that benefits are called *fundraisers* reinforces the connection. Most small organizations sponsor fundraising events as part of their annual development work. While there are many benefits to these events, they are among the least effective ways to raise money. People attending an event may do so because of a friend's invitation to purchase a ticket, or because their company is a sponsor, or because they have a connection to an honoree. Some just like this type of event. These attendees may care little, if at all, about the fine work of the sponsoring organization. Adding to this problem is the fact that fundraising benefits are very labor-intensive and, in many cases, may distract from other, more effective fundraising efforts. In Chapter

Six, Tracy Wayson holds that attendees of benefits should be viewed as "buyers," not donors. She provides a process for using benefits to cultivate and prepare to move those buyers into annual fund donors. It is a new and helpful way to enhance the value of special events.

For many small organizations, fundraising is the most difficult task they face. A lack of visibility in the community and internal weaknesses are magnified when it comes to fundraising. Unlike larger organizations, the work of small organizations often goes unnoticed by people outside its neighborhood or its constituencies. It becomes more difficult to recruit board members and donors from the wider community. Fundraising is a process that is often misunderstood by board members and staff alike. Because fundraising plans flow from the organization's programs, the process should begin with an awareness of the need for those services in their community, a review of other organizations offering similar programs, and the justification for seeking funds to support this work. The work of all organizations, including fundraising, begins with the task of answering these questions: What human or societal need is addressed by this organization? Why does this organization exist? Unfortunately, most organizations spend a great deal of effort explaining *what* they do when donors really need to know *why* they do it. An understanding of the people and communities that benefit from the work of the organization provides the motivation for volunteers and, ultimately, donors to get involved.

Fundraising activities should be undertaken with knowledge of the markets (individuals, foundations, religious institutions, businesses, etc.), how they will reach them (face-to-face solicitation, mailings, proposals, etc.), and what message will have the greatest impact (what part of our program addresses their interest?). Yet in most organizations, fundraising efforts focus on solicitation—who is to be approached, who will solicit, and for what amount. Clearly, the asking part is important, and organizations that don't get around to that part are doomed. However, the program planning, validation of needs and mission, involvement of volunteers, and preparation of the fundraising plan must receive adequate attention in order to increase the likelihood of success in solicitation.

While a diverse fundraising plan is critical to the survival and growth of small organizations, fundraising is often seen as a luxury; something groups get around to after all the other "important" work is tended to. Frequently, one person is hired and given the job of raising money, with little access to board members and no involvement in the annual program planning for the organization. They often are told how much money they have to raise each year based on what the organization *needs*. This goal may be unrealistic, and the onus lies solely with the fundraiser. Many factors determine the success of an annual campaign, such as fundraising history, the strength of programs, skill level and availability of volunteers, and the strength and loyalty of an organization's constituencies.

Another problem arises for the fundraising staff person when other staff do not see fundraising as related to their work. Strong fundraising organizations understand that all staff, from the receptionist to the executive director, have a role to play in the process. How a caller is greeted on the phone, how their gift is acknowledged, and what they see when they tour a program site all affect the relationship that the prospective donor develops with the organization. The culture of the organization is an area over which the fundraiser has little control. Organizations that do not integrate fundraising into all aspects of their work see a high rate of turnover among development professionals. This trend holds true in both large and small nonprofits. The impact on small organizations is deadly: organizations have ceased to exist or dropped programs because there was not enough funding to support them.

In Chapter Seven, Michael Page Miller writes about the strengths and weaknesses of small organizations with advice to trainers, consultants, and funding organization. This final chapter looks at the major challenges that small nonprofits face in their fundraising programs. He advises professionals to take a critical look at an organization's operations and face the hard facts that prevent them from thriving.

Years ago, when I worked in the development office of a large human service organization, the administrative staff was discussing how to best provide training and assistance for the regional staff.

The major training needs were in the areas of public affairs, public relations, and fundraising. After methods to provide assistance in the first two areas were laid out, the executive director suggested that maybe the regional staff could just read a book to help them learn about fundraising. I did my best to contain my outrage and made the case for fundraising to receive attention equal to the other two areas. The idea that simply reading about or just doing fundraising is enough shows the lack of acceptance of fundraising as a complex management process. These views continue to exist today. It would be ludicrous to ask a program staff member to raise the funds to pay their own salary. Yet frequently fundraisers are asked to do just that. They are also asked to accept a percentage of the funds they raise in a year as their annual salary. This request highlights the attitude that fundraising is done in a vacuum and is unrelated to the rest of the organization. These are all challenges that small nonprofits in particular are facing.

This volume was written to stimulate your thoughts, but more importantly, to move you and your organization to action. I urge you to try some of what is being suggested in these pages. Although a book is not enough, it is a good catalyst.

One of the principles of The Fund Raising School is to replace apology for asking with pride in asking. We ask people to give money to support the work of an organization that reflects their values and commitments. Nonprofit organizations do the work that donors may not have the chance to do themselves. They cannot feed the hungry every day, but the local food pantry can and does. Giving a gift to an organization is a way for donors to participate in making their communities better places to live.

Small nonprofits have much to be proud of because their work has such a great impact on the quality of life of so many people. This volume was written to help people within these organizations approach fundraising in the same way they approach their programs—with pride, determination, and passion.

Mary Louise Mussoline
Editor

MARY LOUISE MUSSOLINE *is a fundraising consultant and trainer with many years' experience working with small nonprofit organizations. She is a lead faculty member of The Fund Raising School of the Indiana University Center on Philanthropy.*

*A comprehensive income plan is a breakthrough
strategy that will transform the income side of the
budget into a powerful management tool.*

1

Beyond a hit list: Income planning for small nonprofit organizations

Patricia Wyzbinski, Pam Moore, Scott Gelzer

EVERY NONPROFIT organization needs to raise enough money to
meet budgetary commitments on an annual basis. In doing so, they
must attract the most appropriate resources by the most efficient
means. A systematic approach to financial planning is crucial for
both new and veteran development staff to guide the growth of
their organization's income generation. A comprehensive income
plan will reflect long-term strategies; encompass overall goals and
defined objectives; and assign responsibilities for staff, board, and
other volunteers within a realistic time frame. In an extensive planning initiative, the process provides multiple opportunities to build
on current strengths as well as to explore new opportunities. Monitoring progress throughout the year and evaluating results upon
completion are key components in building success year after year.

Income planning is more than just increasing each line item on
the income side of the annual budget according to an arbitrary or
speculative formula—it is *not* projecting a 10 percent increase
across the board. Nor is it finessing the same old tired benefit into
a moneymaker, applying for another government contract, or
expanding the foundation hit list.

NEW DIRECTIONS FOR PHILANTHROPIC FUNDRAISING, NO. 20, SUMMER 1998 © JOSSEY-BASS PUBLISHERS

Comprehensive income planning is a disciplined approach to detail strategies for a diverse array of revenue sources through organized efforts by the staff, the board of directors, and fundraising volunteers.

The rationale

Many executives, particularly those who operate without the support of development staff, may resist undertaking an involved income planning process because they lack the time. The realities of working in small to mid-sized nonprofit organizations often preclude sustained planning activities. However, it is the experience of the authors after assisting hundreds of nonprofit organizations that the upfront investment of time and effort in an income planning process will reap greater financial rewards as a result.

Indeed, this is a breakthrough strategy for moving the organization to a higher and often more sophisticated level of income generation. Most nonprofit organizations rely on external sources to fund their operations because their ability to earn income is usually not adequate to sustain self-sufficiency. Stated simply, nonprofit organizations always have and forever will need to raise money.

Several typical situations that smaller organizations face identify them as groups that need a more concerted focus on income planning.

Until now, our revenues have consisted of one or two significant government contracts and some personal donations by board directors.

We have gained a wider range of support largely through staff-driven efforts, but we haven't really tapped corporate contributions.

We're losing support from foundations because they've funded us for several years and now want to consider only special projects.

Our agency is ready to expand, but we need to attract more donors who will make larger investments to finance programs over an extended period of time.

In the context of the funding environment, each scenario represents specific challenges that can be addressed through a comprehensive income planning process. This approach begins at the organization's current stage of development, analyzes its patterns of funding, capitalizes on current trends in the resource environment, and devises strategies to position the organization for increased funding.

Planning has benefits

If it involves several parties from the start, the process of developing a plan enhances teamwork. A thorough plan clarifies roles and responsibilities with assignments to appropriate staff members, board directors, and other fundraising volunteers who might be involved through committees or auxiliaries. With a document that projects time frames for completion, all members of the fundraising team understand their part in a coordinated effort. The finished plan instills confidence, demonstrating how all the pieces fit together to achieve common goals. Furthermore, when the plan maps the involvement of the fundraising (or other appropriate) committee and the board of directors, it tends to increase their participation and build ownership for the bottom line.

An organization will usually find that when a thoughtful plan is presented, a donor's confidence in the organization's ability to attract sufficient support for the goals described in proposals is significantly bolstered. Added together, these factors equal greater fundraising success.

Income planning also allows an organization to respond more quickly to a new funding opportunity. Having organized its efforts, a nonprofit executive can efficiently assemble the players and tools to act. Such opportunities do not frequently present themselves to nonprofit organizations—all the more reason to be prepared!

Planning must be coordinated with overall mission and goals

Income planning cannot occur in a vacuum. In fact, it must support the organizational and programmatic goals that uphold the mission. It is assumed that the board of an organization periodically affirms its reason for being and links the programs directly to the fulfill-ment of that purpose. Fundraising strategies merely attract the resources necessary to realize organizational goals; never should a source of funds determine those goals. Smaller nonprofit groups usually lack a diverse revenue base and therefore are more vulner-able to external factors. As one example, some very exciting and creative ventures of the 1960s, 1970s, and 1980s no longer exist because they did not plan beyond the start-up funds (Seltzer, 1987).

The process

Before beginning, gather and review a checklist of documents that will act as a reference tool while you are completing the planning tasks. Documents to include are program plans and administrative goals for the year; audits from the past two years; reports of previ-ous annual campaign activities, special events, or other resource development efforts; current commission statement for the com-mittee charged with fundraising responsibilities; current general operating proposal or case statement; and data or news articles on trends in the fundraising environment.

Staff, committee, and board roles. There are several steps involved in preparing an income plan, with distinct roles for the staff, fundraising committee, and the board of directors.

Usually, the executive director or the *development staff* is charged with the initial gathering of data to conduct an analysis of the income mix and assess environmental trends. The staff is also responsible for drafting fundraising goals and objectives, and com-piling the income plan document for review by a committee.

The *fundraising committee* plays a key role by contributing its members' perspectives and knowledge, especially at the stage of reviewing information. Committee members should discuss and refine the goals and objectives until they are comfortable with a recommendation. They must be committed to "selling" the com-pleted plan to the board so that full participation and agreement with goals and objectives can be achieved. Some organizations may have a resource development committee, combining fundraising and public relations, which will assume these duties.

The *board of directors* has the ultimate responsibility of ensuring that the organization has sufficient resources to achieve its mission. The board must review the income plan recommended by the fundraising committee and decide whether to approve it, send it back to committee for further work, or reject it. In accepting the plan, directors take a critical step in agreeing to implement the fundraising tasks assigned to them. They must also agree to monitor the overall implementation of the plan throughout the year. Regardless of board size or sophistication, fulfilling this leadership and governance role is vital for long-term organizational success.

Income diversification. One assumption underlying this approach is that a diversified income base represents the most stable fiscal position for any nonprofit organization. A look at the trends of the past decade—corporate restructuring, mergers, and devolution—illustrates the importance of not relying on any single type of funding, no matter how attractive it may be. A broad income base encompasses complementary proportions of contributed and earned revenues, with diverse sources represented within each of the funding categories.

In addition to foundations and corporations, there are many distinct types of contributed funding. Of course, there are also many specific sources within each type.

Step 1: Analyzing the income mix

The income planning effort begins—as all good plans do—with an analysis of the past. Using a list of possible income sources, staff should chart the amounts of income received over the past several years and the percentage of the overall budget these amounts represent. These figures should be culled from the annual audit; however, the audit usually does not provide adequate detail for specific income categories. In this case, the staff should review interim financial statements or obtain a supplementary schedule detailing the income sources from the auditors.

Government	Federated Campaigns	Individuals
Federal	United Way	Board of directors
State	Combined Federal	Annual donors
County	Campaign	Major gifts
Municipal	United Jewish Appeal	Memorials/celebrations
	Alternative workplace	Bequests
	solicitations	Planned giving donors
Community	Special events	Earned income
Local businesses	Annual meetings	Memberships
Neighborhood organi-	Benefits (from *a* to *z*)	Subscriptions
zations	Seminars or confer-	Fees, admissions,
Religious institutions	ences	tuition
Civic groups		Contracted sales
Professional associa-		Product sales
tions		Investments
Unions		Program-related
		events
		Sponsorships
		Business ventures

Once the historical portion of the spreadsheet is complete, an analysis of the figures will reveal patterns in the income mix and highlight sources that are yet untapped or underdeveloped. Focused discussion involving the executive director and the fundraising committee should review past efforts with every type of contributed and earned income. This review will guide the group toward formulating a more balanced yet realistic income mix. The board should approve financial goals that diversify the income so that a more stable base can be achieved.

For example, a social service organization may have averaged 85 percent contributed and 15 percent earned income over the past two years. Within the contributed sources, the analysts observe that the organization has relied primarily on government and foundation grants and gained relatively less support from individuals and the local community. The discussion concerning these findings might also recall a two-year effort to solicit civic groups and professional associations that ended in FY 1996 because it yielded poor results. Yet neighboring churches and local businesses, which had not been considered previously, offer potential because both are now represented on the board. In dissecting the past several special events, it may become apparent that the annual benefit has peaked at $10,000 net, but possibilities for adding another revenue stream to it or a smaller event to the roster might be of interest.

The board of this organization might realistically decide that in the coming year it would like to shift the income mix to 80 percent contributed, 20 percent earned. Within that overall formula, a campaign designed to solicit sponsorships from local businesses to underwrite program development or expansion might be pursued.

Additional special events could be organized by young adults recruited from nearby churches. The organization could also establish a three-year goal of becoming 70 percent contributed and 30 percent earned, or whatever balance is believed to be more stable and attainable.

In contrast, the balance between contributed and earned revenues could be reversed if the example highlighted figures from a performing arts organization, a health center, school, or any other type of nonprofit organization with a greater ability to generate program fees.

Step 2: Researching philanthropic trends

Before making a commitment to devise new strategies, there is more homework to do. To formulate the best plan, the executive director must gauge the organization's capacity to raise funds within the context of general philanthropic trends. This understanding may be gained by analyzing the annual reports of peer organizations as well as conducting more formal research by reading relevant trade journals such as *Nonprofit Times* and *The Chronicle of Philanthropy*. The intended outcome of this exercise is to take a snapshot of philanthropy at both the national and local levels.

These fact-finding activities usually are assigned to development staff. Fundraising committee members could be instrumental in talking to peers who serve on other nonprofit boards or in reflecting on the general state of philanthropy. If feasible, a few interviews with area foundation staff or individual philanthropists could also supplement the printed material.

At the national level, staff investigators could easily determine that government funding is expected to continue to tighten although creative development staff may be able to unearth new opportunities or discreet funding initiatives. Individuals continue to contribute the major portion of all privately donated dollars, but that giving is often linked to their religious institutions. Although foundations have benefitted from stock market growth, resulting in larger amounts of money available for grants, corporations are looking to employees and sponsorship opportunities in order to increase the impact of their social investments.

Certainly, it can be useful to analyze national trends. For instance, U.S. 1996 contributions were up 7.3 percent over 1995 and individual gifts dwarf all other private revenue sources. However, for nonprofit organizations based in the Milwaukee, Wisconsin, area, it is far more useful to understand that local giving is rising faster than the national norm (Public Policy Forum, 1997). Sources of valuable information to be gleaned through a wider lens may include community foundations, the United Way, or the regional association of grant makers.

Armed with a thorough understanding of historical funding patterns and potential environmental trends, the executive director is now ready to support organizational strategies by determining financial goals, detailing objectives, and establishing deadlines.

Step 3: Formulating strategies, goals, and objectives

In general, determining strategies, goals, and objectives should follow a planning process of building on the fundraising track record, brainstorming new ideas, assessing feasibility, and recommending those which are perceived to be realistic.

The organization's strategic or long-range plan may provide further guidance in compiling the income plan. For example, if one of the longer-term strategies was to build support for the organization within the corporate community, it would be important to delineate goals and objectives to reinforce that strategic direction, such as, "attract at least five new corporate grants" and "negotiate two corporate sponsorships each year."

General parameters for goals must be adapted to reflect the uniqueness of each income source. An organization may want to decrease the percentage of the operating budget for a specific source; rarely does it want to reduce the total amount raised from that source. It is far more likely to balance its income mix by increasing other types of funding. Hence, maintaining contributions or earnings will be the lowest degree to which an organization will aspire.

Other goals will address expanding the number of donors or increasing the amounts that they contribute. For example, within the area of foundations, an organization may have a continuum of goals:

- To maintain giving levels at 80 percent of the current funders
- To attract funding from at least five additional local foundations
- To solicit two regional or national foundations
- To host a donor cultivation event to recognize current foundation supporters and introduce the organization to prospective funders

With individual contributors, the goals may focus on expanding the donor base as well as increasing the level of giving:

- To increase the individual donor base by 15 percent with an average gift of $50
- To recruit the top 10 percent of current annual givers to a $500 roundtable
- To conduct a major donor campaign attracting at least five donors at the $1,000 level

Earned income is a familiar term in the nonprofit lexicon as organizations have sought to have greater control over their fiscal stability. At the very least, organizations need to have goals that result in optimal management of their assets through such strategies as interest-bearing accounts and secured investments (Stevens and Anderson, 1997). Many organizations earn revenues from fees, admissions, memberships or subscriptions, and contracted services. For more entrepreneurial managers, earned-income ventures, which are mission-based, may represent new "fundraising" strategies. On matters concerning unrelated business income, the organization should consult its corporate attorney or accountant.

Whatever the income source, formulating goals and objectives that undergird the longer-term strategies should begin with the staff and be enhanced by the fundraising committee. Ultimately, they must be embraced by the board of directors. On a cautionary note, organizations should take care not to be carried away in the fervor of planning and overestimate their capabilities to implement sound ideas. Many organizations find that they must spread their excitement over at least a two-year period.

The product

The income plan should be documented in a format that is succinct but detailed enough to serve as a useful management tool throughout the year.

Sample table of contents of income plan

Plan summary
    Overview of fiscal stability
    Changes in environment having an impact on the year or years covered by the plan
    Financial strategies for the fiscal year
Funding history
Environmental trends
Income mix analysis and projections for one to three years
Goals and objectives for each income source, with responsibilities and time frames for implementation
Administrative support needed to implement the plan

The introduction should provide the context for significant proposed changes in income and present a summary of the outcomes intended as a result of implementing the plan. This section of the plan not only acts as an abstract or executive summary but also should entice the reader to play a role in achieving the outcomes.

The document then presents the organization's funding history as well as philanthropic trends in its environment. Depending on the extent of the research, both of these sections may consist of a few paragraphs or several pages.

The income mix analysis is most helpful if presented in table format, depicting a five-year spread including two past years of audited income sources, current budget commitments, and two years of income projections. (See Exhibit 1.1.)

The bulk of the plan should be in a standard format. The dollar achievements and projections form the context, and goals, objectives, assignments, and time frames are listed *for each income area.* It is usual to identify two to four goals per type of funding, with four to eight objectives per goal. (See Exhibit 1.2.)

It is particularly helpful to begin each page with a list of the amounts raised during the past two years, the current amount budgeted, and future projections, thereby providing a financial context. These figures can be culled from the income mix analysis that has already been presented in overview fashion.

Specific sources should be listed within each income area, with separate aims for each. Foundations and corporations should be listed separately, with the amount of the request projected for each. Keeping these two source types distinct is important because corporate funding often attracts other corporations. A simple way to delineate the two is by determining the origination of the money, that is, a foundation endowment or corporate profits allocated to the entity.

For the remainder of each section, the total dollar amount is divided into the specific categories, with notations indicating the actual source. Then the specific goal for the income category is stated and objectives to achieve that goal listed. For each objective, staff, committee, or board should be assigned and a time frame for completion determined.

Administrative systems

Behind every successful fundraising effort are administrative systems that support the team with information, material, and technology. It

Exhibit 1.1. Income plan: Summary of past, current, and projected income

Fiscal year ending: (month) Source	FY '96 (audit) Amount	%	FY '97 (audit) Amount	%	FY '98 (operating budget) Amount	%	FY '99 (projections) Amount	%	FY '00 (projections) Amount	%
Contributed income										
Government										
Foundations										
Corporations										
Federated campaigns										
Individuals/general public										
Board of directors										
Major donors										
Community/local businesses										
Religious institutions										
Civic/prof./comm. orgs.										
Special events										
Subtotal contributed income										
Earned income										
Admissions/tuitions/fees										
Sponsorships										
Memberships/subscriptions										
Contracted services										
Product sales										
Investments/interest										
Business revenues										
Subtotal earned income										
Grand total										

Exhibit 1.2. Income plan: Goals and objectives by income area

Foundations

Achievement	FY '96	$96,198
Achievement	FY '97	$109,224
Goal	FY '98	$125,000
Goal	FY '99	$145,000
Goal	FY '00	$150,000

Strategy: To retain at least 80 percent of current foundation support and secure funding from at least five new foundations per year, with one having a regional or national interest.

Foundation sources (Attached list to be updated annually)

Goals and objectives	Assignment	Time frame
Goal #1: To retain at least 80 percent of current foundation support		
Objective a: Investigate the potential of continuing support from current funders.	Development/executive director	Feb. annually
Objective b: Determine funders' criteria for additional funding.	Development staff	Feb. annually
Objective c: Initiate plans, activities, and report deadlines for completion of criteria.	Development staff	Ongoing
Objective d: Submit required renewal requests to repeat funders.	Development staff	Per deadlines
Objective e: Follow up each proposal with a phone call or site visit.	Board director	Two weeks after submittal
Goal #2: To attract funding from five new foundations each year		
Objective a: Identify and research at least twenty new foundations.	Development staff	Jan. and Aug. annually
Objective b: Send letters of introductions and request foundation guidelines.	Development staff	Jan. and Aug. annually
Objective c: Call prospective donors to establish a personal relationship and assess their interest in our organization.	Development director	As appropriate
Objective d: Submit proposals relevant to potential funders (program-specific or general operating).	Development staff	Per deadlines
Objective e: Call each prospective funder who is reviewing a proposal to answer questions and highlight recent activities.	Board director and development director	Two weeks after submittal
Objective f: Thank each funder appropriately.	Board/staff	On receipt of grant

Source: Management Cornerstones.

is recommended that administrative goals also be set to ensure that the organization is fully capable of achieving its income goals. For example, a research and record keeping system must be in place to identify potential sources and track all contributions. There is nothing more embarrassing for the fundraising team than to approach a potential donor only to learn that that donor has given in the past—but was never properly acknowledged and there is no record of any prior contact! Likewise, attractive and complete materials must be available for the solicitation team. These may range from a two-page letter of inquiry to a brochure or annual report to the case statement or grant application. Another subject to include in the management goals is professional training for staff or the board in conquering their fears of fundraising. If the administrative systems are not able to support fundraising efforts, include goals and objectives to enhance administrative capacity in the income plan.

Implementation

Once the board of directors approves the income plan (ideally, prior to the start of the new fiscal year), the plan should become a useful tool for monitoring progress and making adjustments as necessary on a quarterly basis. Many groups have found it helpful to produce a monthly calendar in addition to the plan, a calendar that organizes the plan's objectives chronologically. In this way, development staff can see at a glance what needs to be accomplished and whether it is being completed in the designated time frame. During their regular meetings, the fundraising committee keeps abreast of progress and works with the staff to troubleshoot any problems.

At every board meeting, the chair of the fundraising committee should be prepared by the staff to report on overall fundraising progress, placing particular emphasis on the status of the board's fulfillment of its responsibilities. When it is time for the organizational evaluation at the end of the fiscal year, successes and challenges are apparent within the context of the income plan. The staff, fundraising committee, and board of directors are all able to review fundraising efforts at the level of detail appropriate for each group and to formulate evaluative opinions.

Conclusion

Moving beyond the hit list and establishing a comprehensive income plan, particularly for the first time, represents hard work on the part of many. Yet it's not so different from the usual demands of fundraising; it simply organizes the work in a coordinated fashion that enhances teamwork by getting everyone involved *literally* on the same page. There's no question that the first year is the most difficult because it may require a change in the organizational mind-set in addition to the hard work of designing the plan, developing it, and preparing financial data in a slightly different way. However, by the second year, the basic planning functions and all systems are in place for doing it all over again. As the organization becomes more adept at implementing its income plan, fundraising activities are likely to become increasingly more sophisticated *and* successful.

References

Management Cornerstones. Various copyrighted tools and handouts. Milwaukee, Wisc.: Management Cornerstones, 1985–1998.

Public Policy Forum. *Report Card on Charitable Giving.* Milwaukee, Wisc.: Milwaukee Foundation, 1997.

Seltzer, M. *Securing Your Organization's Future.* New York: Foundation Center, 1987.

Stevens, S. K., and Anderson, L. M. *All the Way to the Bank: Smart Money Management for Tomorrow's Nonprofit.* St. Paul, Minn.: Stevens Group, 1997.

PATRICIA WYZBINSKI *is president of Management Cornerstones, Inc., a Milwaukee-based consulting firm that provides technical assistance to enable nonprofit organizations to be effectively and efficiently managed. She has more than twenty-three years' experience as a management consultant to nonprofit organizations.*

PAM MOORE *is a consultant with Management Cornerstones, Inc. She has consulted with hundreds of organizations in all management areas. She has a strong interest in filmmaking and has managed a film post house.*

SCOTT GELZER *is vice president of Management Cornerstones, Inc. His areas of concentration are program planning and evaluation, employment and training projects, fundraising, earned income, and business ventures for nonprofit organizations.*

A number of key practices that reinforce one another lay the groundwork for general board effectiveness and position the board for effective fundraising as well.

2

The board of directors: Foundation for success

Frank Martinelli

EVERY NONPROFIT ORGANIZATION must have a board of directors. In addition to being a legal requirement, a well-informed and well-trained board is absolutely essential to an organization's success. An effective board of directors has a clear understanding of its roles and responsibilities. Board members, in effect, own the organization. They are the final policymakers and they employ staff.

Roles and responsibilities of the board

The board has three main areas of responsibility: planning and policy development; community and organizational development; and fundraising and support development.

The first area of responsibility—planning and policy development—includes determining the mission and vision that charts the future direction of the organization. The board usually accomplishes this through its leadership and participation in strategic

NEW DIRECTIONS FOR PHILANTHROPIC FUNDRAISING, NO. 20, SUMMER 1998 © JOSSEY-BASS PUBLISHERS

planning. The board develops policy in response to major issues confronting the organization or those that in the future will have significant impact on the agency and its constituencies. Also falling within this area is the board's monitoring the performance of agency programs, products, and services.

The second area—community and organizational development—includes broadening the organization's base of support in the community; interacting with the community to bring new issues, opportunities, and community needs to the attention of the organization; and maintaining accountability to the public, funders, members, and clients. It also includes training and developing current and new leaders within the board and committees, and assuring that the same development is occurring within the professional staff through the leadership of the executive director.

The third area—fundraising and support development—includes giving personal time and money; developing donors, members, and supporters; leading and supporting fundraising campaigns and events; and maintaining accountability to donors and funders.

The three areas are closely linked. If the board is going to make decisions that reflect the true interests and needs of the organization's constituents, its members must be in tune with those constituents and the wider community of which they are a part. If the board is expected to raise funds to support the programs and services of the organization, then board members must be involved in planning and decision making in meaningful ways so that they feel a strong sense of individual and collective ownership. If the organization is counting on board members to raise funds from the community, then those board members need to maintain relationships with individuals and institutions in that community.

Barriers to board effectiveness

There are a number of reasons why some boards don't function effectively. Taken together, these factors can provide a checklist for assessing a board and identifying problem areas. Examining these barriers to board effectiveness is the first step in revitalizing an existing board or in building from scratch.

Temptation to micromanage

Almost everyone can share hair-raising stories about boards that spend untold hours discussing trivial subjects while neglecting major agenda items deserving their careful deliberation. It is critical that the board focuses its attention on items of true importance to the organization. To do this, it must avoid the temptation to micromanage or meddle in matters that are more appropriately handled by the professional staff. The average board, meeting monthly for two hours, has approximately twenty-four hours of meeting time each year in which to make all major decisions as well as address critical issues that come before it unannounced. It is simply impossible to do an effective job within that period of meeting time if even a few hours are wasted on trivial things.

Ineffective nominating committee

The nominating committee keeps the board vital; it builds new leadership and shapes the future. The work of the nominating committee has lasting impact on an organization because it determines who the organization's leaders will be for many years to come. Thus, the nominating committee should be well organized and have a clear sense of recruiting priorities and expectations for individual board members, especially in the area of fundraising. But these elements are often missing. If the nominating committee is poorly organized—or nonexistent—then board members are not likely to have a good understanding of the organization and their role as board members.

Failure to keep board members connected

Most people join a board because they feel passionate about the organization's mission. Board members need to be kept informed about new program developments and given examples of how the services of the agency are having an impact on its mission. There must be a balance between giving the board insight into program operations without inviting micromanagement.

No rotation plan

If the same people serve year after year, there is no way for new blood and new ideas to flow into the board. Despite their sense of commitment, the same people will make the organization a "closed corporation." Rotation prevents the possessiveness that sometimes characterizes self-perpetuating boards. In a time of rapid change, new people—who bring a new perspective—will promote creativity and innovation in board decision making.

Failure to remove unproductive members

People who are not carrying out their commitments as board members become major blocks to overall board effectiveness. Organizations need a process for evaluating the performance of board members and making recommendations regarding their future service with the board.

Small size

Sometimes a board is ineffective because it is simply too small. Considering the significant responsibilities of a board, it's easy to see why an adequate number of people are needed to do the work. Although it is difficult to specify an appropriate size for all boards, in general a board should range in number from eleven to twenty-one members. A board needs enough members to lead and form the core of the committees and share in the other work of the board. Sufficient numbers are also needed if the board is to reflect the desired diversity and assure that there are a range of viewpoints to spur innovation and creativity in planning and decision making.

Lack of functioning committee structure

The lack of a well-functioning committee structure leads to failed performance. Although it is true that major decisions are made in board meetings, it is also true that most of the work that supports this decision making occurs at the committee level.

No strategic plan

If the organization lacks a strategic plan that provides clear direction—so critical in this period of rapid change—the board can spend significant amounts of time talking about topics that simply don't matter. The organization also needs a long-range service delivery and financial development plan that will advance the strategic plan.

No orientation plan

Deliberate thought is rarely given to the matter of blending new and old board members into a well-functioning team. Also problematic is the lack of a formal plan of board training and education to assure that the level of the board's skills and knowledge is continually upgraded.

Some of these problems likely sound painfully familiar; all are preventable. The following paragraphs present basic tools and techniques to help boards to address these barriers.

Building a more effective board is a process. Things don't change overnight in organizations. It takes commitment on the part of the leaders of a board to make change happen. The experience of nonprofits suggests that it can take two to five years to create an effective, self-renewing board. But if board members are willing to make the commitment and apply the proven techniques that follow, dramatic improvements are possible almost immediately. Furthermore, if you think that a serious board development effort is only for large organizations, think again. Such a process is even more important for small nonprofits that rely more heavily on committed board leadership.

The board recruitment and nominations process

The first board development practice—and by far the most important—is having in place a board recruitment and nominations process. In contrast to the typical short-term recruitment process, which focuses narrowly on filling anticipated board vacancies for the current year, this process helps assure that there is a long-range plan for board leadership development. The long-range plan centers on the following questions:

- Who will be serving on and leading the board over the next five years?
- What is our plan to scout board leadership talent for the future?
- How will we go about fostering and developing future board leadership?

What we're really talking about here is extending the time line for board development and recruitment activities. In many organizations, board recruitment and nominations activities are ad hoc in nature. Typical bylaws describe a process in which the board's president appoints a nominations committee whose short-term task is to recruit candidates to fill a specified number of vacancies at the upcoming annual meeting. In contrast, the following are characteristics of a long-range leadership development process.

Year-round committee

Because board recruitment and nomination are such important activities, they should be year-round committee functions instead of part of the traditional ad hoc nominations process. Reflecting this long-range focus, many boards are changing the committee name from "Nominations Committee" to "Board Development Committee" because developing leaders means more than nominating people to serve on the board. It truly is a year-round function: prospecting, contacting, recruiting, supporting, providing ongoing training, and evaluating.

Link to the strategic plan

Board recruitment and development activities need to be matched with the new requirements and demands of the strategic plan. The ideal time to do this is right after the strategic planning process has been completed. The board reviews the mission, vision, goals, and strategies and then determines any new skills, knowledge, personal contacts, and other attributes future board members should possess in order for the board to do its part in advancing the strategic plan.

Profile of the current board

At the same time, the current makeup of the board should be analyzed. The board development committee can create a profile of the current board using a matrix designed for this purpose. Arranged along the top of the matrix are key factors that define sought-after expertise, knowledge, skills, and experience, along with relevant demographic factors. The names of current board members are listed down the side of the matrix.

Focused recruiting priorities

By reviewing the agency's strategic plan as well as the profile of the current board's strengths and weaknesses, the board development committee identifies the gap between the skills and knowledge needed and what board members currently possess. Based on this analysis, the board development committee can set clear recruiting priorities for future board recruitment.

Written job description

For a board to operate successfully, each member must understand and accept the specific duties and responsibilities that come with the job. It helps to develop a written statement of agreement, which serves as a job description and clarifies board responsibilities. A sample board member job description is presented in Exhibit 2.1. In very clear language, this job description sets forth the organization's expectations of its board members. The most effective job descriptions state in behavioral terms precisely what board members are expected to do.

This written job description, which should be periodically reviewed and updated by the board of directors, is the critical tool in recruiting new board members. Like anyone contemplating a serious volunteer commitment, prospective board members want to know what is expected of them and want an estimate of the

Exhibit 2.1. Sample board member position description

1. Attend monthly meetings of the board, which last approximately two hours each. Be accessible for personal contact between board meetings.

2. Provide leadership to board committees. Each board member is expected to serve as an active member of at least one committee. This requires at least eight committee meetings per year plus additional time to complete committee tasks. The following committees are currently in existence: resource development, strategic planning, board development, personnel, finance, and executive.

3. Commit time to developing financial resources for the organization. This includes making a personally meaningful financial gift as well as supporting other fund development activities of the organization in a manner appropriate for board members.

4. Responsibly review and act on committee recommendations brought to the board for action.

5. Prepare in advance for decision making and policy formation at board meetings; take responsibility for self-education on the major issues before the board.

6. Participate in the annual board development and planning retreat, usually held on the second Saturday of October each year.

7. In general, use personal and professional skills, relationships, and knowledge for the advancement of the organization.

I am aware that this board member position description is an expression of good faith and provides a common ground from which board members can operate. Additional information on organizational mission and board responsibilities is contained in the board orientation materials and bylaws, which I have read.

required time. Organizations should avoid the temptation to down-play board membership responsibilities. New board members will eventually find out what the true expectations are and if they are different from what they were told before coming onto the board, the organization is in trouble!

The executive committee

Another critical element in board effectiveness is a functioning executive committee. In most organizations, the executive committee consists of the four executive officers of the board: president, vice president, secretary, and treasurer. Sometimes other members of the board are included as well; for example, chairs of the standing committees or at-large members from the board may be included to assure representation of diverse viewpoints.

The executive committee plays three critical roles:

Planning the agenda of board meetings. It is the responsibility of the executive committee to meet regularly with the executive director before board meetings to develop the meetings' agendas.

Making decisions on behalf of the full board. Between the regular meetings of the board, the executive committee can make decisions that can't wait until the next regular board meeting or decide on matters over which the full board has delegated it authority. In both cases, the executive committee receives its authority from the full board and reports on its decisions at the subsequent meeting of the board.

Serving as a communication link with other members of the board, especially the committee chairs. In order to be effective, the board must foster communication among its members between regular meetings. The executive committee plays a vital role in ensuring that this happens by using telephone, fax, and e-mail.

To facilitate its work, the executive committee should meet on a regular basis. For example, if the board holds its regular meetings on a monthly basis, the executive committee might also meet each month in between the regular board meetings.

The president and executive director should develop an agenda for the executive committee in advance of its meetings. They should begin by identifying agenda items that the executive committee will handle. These items are then placed on the executive committee's meeting agenda as action items. In placing such items in this category, board president and executive director are assuming, based on past practice as well as relevant bylaw language and board policy, that such items are appropriate for executive committee decision making. The next agenda category includes those items that would be appropriate for executive committee discussion or referral to the full board as action items or as information items. In this instance, the board president and executive director are judging that the executive committee lacks authority to act directly. The executive committee's discussion of such items during its meeting may lead to recommendations for future action by the board as a whole, but the executive committee will stop short of making a decision on its own.

A third category of agenda items includes those that are offered to executive committee members for their information only; these items don't require action by either the executive committee or the board as a whole, but the board president and executive director consider the information important enough to share it with other executive committee members.

When an executive committee agenda is organized in this manner, the members will use their meeting time more effectively and efficiently, resulting in decisions on matters that are appropriate for their action. More important, the members will lay the groundwork for effective decision making by the board as a whole when they review and, if appropriate, make recommendations for action on items to be handled by the full board of directors. They will also avoid spending unnecessary time on information items that require no real discussion or deliberation.

As a result of such a meeting process, the executive committee can construct an agenda for the full board meeting that prioritizes action items. It can be seen that by taking care of its own work in an effective way, the executive committee facilitates effective decision-

Exhibit 2.2. Executive committee agenda planning form

Date _____

Items for executive committee action/decision:

1.

2.

3.

Items for executive committee discussion and/or referral to full board as action items (with or without recommendation) or as informational items:

1.

2.

3.

Items for executive committee information only:

1.

2.

3.

Key items for next board meeting:

1.

2.

3.

making by the board as a whole. Exhibit 2.2 shows an executive committee meeting agenda planning form.

The committee structure

Although the executive committee is important, it's only one part of the total committee structure. Effective committees are indispensable. They do the bulk of the organization's work, freeing the full board for attention to matters like long-range financial planning and policy development.

An effective committee structure plays the following crucial roles:

- It helps to increase the involvement of board members because it gives them an opportunity to use their skills and experience.
- It provides a training ground for future leaders—both for individuals who are currently board members and for those who are not but may be asked to serve on the board in the future.
- It increases the visibility and outreach of the organization by including individuals who are not board members on committees.
- It provides a means for information to flow from the community, clients, and line staff to the board.
- It gives committee members the chance to discuss emerging issues in some depth.

A committee's effectiveness stems from several elements.

Clear description of its work and accountability to the board. Accountability begins with a clear written description of what the board expects from the committee. This description serves as a guide for the chair and members alike. It should summarize the purpose of the committee, its composition and selection procedure, and the specific duties of the committee. A sample of a fund development committee description is presented in Exhibit 2.3.

There should also be an effort to link the committee description with relevant strategic plan language. Again using the fund development committee as an example, the committee description would reflect a major goal and supporting strategies that address the issue of agency funding. Under the umbrella of the funding goal and strategies, committee leadership would develop an annual fundraising strategy and supporting work plan in line with the strategic goal. This work plan would contain objectives incorporating measurable outcomes, and these measurable outcomes would be the basis for regular reporting of the committee to the board as a whole. Regardless of the approach used, it is important that the board clearly communicate to all its committees the kind of reporting it expects and with what frequency.

Exhibit 2.3. Sample fundraising committee description

General purpose

The Fundraising Committee is commissioned by and answerable to the Board of Directors to assume primary responsibility for raising nongrant funds to meet the budget of the organization. The Board of Directors, in consultation with the Fundraising Committee, Finance Committee, and Executive Director, will determine the fundraising goal for the Fundraising Committee.

Appointments and composition

1. Appointments of the chair and members of the Fundraising Committee shall be made annually by the president of the Board with the advice and consent of the Board in accordance with the bylaws.
2. Other members may be appointed and need not be members of the Board of Directors, subject to the conditions stated in the bylaws. These members are appointed annually by the president of the Board, who may consult the chair of the committee.

Responsibilities

1. Develop an annual fundraising plan that will generate the funds needed to meet the fundraising goal.
2. Develop the necessary subcommittee systems to carry out the activities that are part of the annual fundraising plan.
3. Supervise the functions of the subcommittees.
4. Develop a plan for involving Board members in the fundraising activities of the organization.
5. Pursue new fundraising projects, activities, and ideas for possible use in the future.
6. Annually submit objectives as part of the planning and budgeting process.
7. Annually evaluate the committee's work and objectives and report on these to the Board of Directors.
8. Report to the Board of Directors at regular meetings of the Board in a manner determined by the Board.

A mix of board and nonboard members. Each standing committee is generally composed of a core of five to eight members, who can be a mix of board members and individual who are not board members. The group should be recruited with a specific question in mind: What tasks is the committee responsible for and who among our members and supporters possess the skills and experience needed to complete those tasks?

A match between members' experience and committee needs. As when recruiting any volunteers, the organization should make every effort to match the needs and requirements of the committee with the skills, knowledge, and interests of prospective committee members. In many cases, as part of the recruitment process, prospective board members will be given information about the board committee structure and suggestions about where they might best fit. For example, a prospective board member who has much skill and experience in fundraising would most likely be asked to serve on the fund development committee. In the end, however, regardless of the preferences of board leaders, the individual board members should be able to select the committee assignment that they feel will best meet their needs while at the same time meet the needs of the organization.

A chair who knows how to lead. In general, the committee chair should be a board member. This helps to assure that the leadership of the committee is "in sync" with that of the board as a whole. In seeking an effective chair, a few qualities are needed: content knowledge and experience that is relevant to the work of the committee as well as proven leadership and people skills, which will be essential if the committee is to work effectively. Depending on the size of the organization, the committee chair prepares agendas for the meetings, assigns responsibilities to committee members, and does some follow-up to make sure assigned work is being done by members. In some instances, paid professional staff may be assigned to assist the committee chair.

Well-run meetings. The last element of committee effectiveness is well-run meetings. In a sense, if a committee embodies the other indicators of effectiveness—that is, if it has a clear description of its work and direct accountability to the board; a good mix of board and nonboard members; a solid match between the interests, skills, and experience of individual members and the needs and requirements of the committee; and a chair who knows how to lead—then it has the makings for excellent committee meetings. However, it will still be important to provide meeting space that matches the needs of the group and a written meeting agenda and to mail any necessary information to members in advance of the meeting.

As part of the overall board education and training program, the organization should also be prepared to provide training to committee members to help them sharpen their skills.

Board self-evaluation process

Another key component in building an effective board is establishing a process for annual self-evaluation of the board. A well-planned recruitment process and an effective committee structure lays the groundwork for improved board performance. However, every so often the board as a whole needs to step back and look at itself. A process for board self-evaluation will help to maintain a high level of performance. It happens informally when directors get together and talk about individual and board concerns, but a formal process is also necessary. It should be noted that we are speaking of self-evaluation. In order to ensure board member commitment to the process, it is important that the board's members are actors in the assessment process rather than the passive recipients of someone else's evaluation of their performance.

An effective board evaluation process includes the following features:

Annual process

An effective process for self-evaluation of the board will be conducted on a regular, yearly basis. A good time is midway into the board year—by then, board members have had an opportunity to demonstrate their commitment and enough time remains to take corrective action if necessary.

Two-way communication

To gain support for the process, the evaluation should be viewed as a vehicle for providing feedback on performance to individual board members and soliciting feedback from individual members on the performance of a board as a whole and the level of support that they receive from their leaders and staff. A thorough evaluation would cover two areas: individual board member performance and board and committee operations as a whole. Each board member should first be asked to assess his or her own performance as a board member in critical areas such as input into policy and decision making, committee participation, and fundraising (see Exhibit 2.4). Board members should also be asked if any factors have helped or hindered their performance. Finally, they should be asked what they would need to maintain or increase their level of commitment.

Follow-through

An effective evaluation process will also lead to concrete plans for corrective action including a commitment on the part of the board to follow through so that the results of an evaluation process lead to measurable improvements in board performance.

Board member accountability

The results of this assessment are then used by the president and executive committee to determine which board members deserve positive feedback for acceptable performance and which board members, because of inadequate performance, need to be reminded of their responsibilities. Finally, an effective evaluation process will relate directly to the overall board recruitment and nominations process. For example, a board member who has not followed through on commitments is unlikely to be asked by the board development committee to run for a second term even though the bylaws may allow for this.

Exhibit 2.4. Individual board member evaluation form

Your name: _____

Part 1. Are you satisfied with your performance as a board member in the following areas? (Check spaces that apply
below.)

	Very good	Adequate	Needs work
Input in policy development and decision making	_____	_____	_____
Committee participation	_____	_____	_____
Fundraising	_____	_____	_____
Community outreach	_____	_____	_____
Other _____	_____	_____	_____

Part 2. What factors contributed to your performance or lack of
performance in the areas above? (Please be specific.)

Part 3. What do you need from the organization to maintain or
increase your level of board commitment?

Part 4. Do you have any other comments or suggestions that will
help the board increase its effectiveness?

Just-in-time board orientation

Another component of board effectiveness is training and orientation provided in a timely manner. It can sometimes take new board members several months and even a full year before they begin to function effectively in their role as board members. In order to speed up the learning curve, some boards are beginning to deliver board orientation on a just-in-time basis. New board members are given an advance orientation program to prepare them to hit the ground running. Even before a prospective board member is voted onto the board, he or she will receive detailed information about the organization, the workings of the board, expectations for individual members, and other vital information. An effective just-in-time orientation program will also focus on the strategic plan of the organization. It is critical that prospective board members be familiar with the mission, vision, major goals, and strategies of the organization. After the new board member has been brought onto a board, additional information and training can be provided so that to the greatest extent possible new board members will be able to participate in their first meeting with confidence. In this way their productivity is assured.

Summary

An effective board of directors is built on a number of key practices. The first is a thoughtful nominations and recruitment process that is seen as part of a broader effort to identify, involve, and develop board leadership. The second is an executive committee that facilitates effective decision making on the part of the board as a whole. The third practice is establishment of a committee structure. The fourth is a process for periodic evaluation of board performance. In all, these processes and structures reinforce one another and lay the groundwork for board effectiveness in general and position the board for effective fundraising as well.

Resources

Carver, J. *Boards That Make a Difference.* San Francisco: Jossey-Bass, 1997.

Kleinsasser, H. (ed.). *Board Member Orientation: Strategies for Nonprofit Executives.* Frederick, Md.: Aspen, 1995.

Learning Institute for Nonprofit Organizations. [http://www.uwex.edu/li]

Moyers, R. (ed.). *Board Member.* Washington, D.C.: National Center for Nonprofit Boards (all issues), 1998.

Muehrcke, J. (ed.). *Nonprofit World.* Madison, WI: Society for Nonprofit Organizations (all issues), 1998.

National Center for Nonprofit Boards. [http://ncnb.org/home.html]

Society for Nonprofit Organizations. [http://danenet.wicip.org/snpo]

FRANK MARTINELLI *is president of the Center for Public Skills Training in Milwaukee, where he specializes in strategic planning, board development, and organizational learning.*

Effectively employing volunteers at all levels of the development effort can be a practical way for small organizations to increase productivity, proficiency, and ultimately, revenue.

3

Staffing fundraising in small organizations

Marissa C. Weaver

MANY FUNDRAISERS in small organizations suffer from stress, fatigue, or burnout. In some instances, one person may function as the development officer, public relations manager, and executive director—and provide additional coverage as the secretary, janitor, and computer technician as well. This is often the dilemma if you believe that the head of a small not-for-profit must wear all of the proverbial hats. By their nature, small organizations usually cannot afford the luxury of large development departments whereas in reality staffing the development effort requires just that—staff. However, with solid planning and management, a small organization can develop and use a volunteer staff program to mirror creatively the efficiency of a large development office.

In a development-driven volunteer program, volunteers fall into one of three categories: on-site staff, ad hoc working committees, and board members. To implement such a program successfully, the executive director or development director must move away from working in a hands-on capacity to operating as a facilitator or

NEW DIRECTIONS FOR PHILANTHROPIC FUNDRAISING, NO. 20, SUMMER 1998 © JOSSEY-BASS PUBLISHERS

trainer. This is not to be confused with transferring responsibility and accountability, because ultimately the success of an annual fund drive and other campaigns rests squarely on the shoulders of the executive director. In addition, just as when managing paid staff, it is necessary to make certain that volunteers' needs and concerns are dealt with. Recruiting and training individuals while providing ongoing support, feedback, and recognition are all part of effective volunteer management.

Volunteer staff: A creative approach

Volunteer is a very loose term when used in this context. Many so-called volunteers who work daily at nonprofit organizations actually are paid wages or receive some other form of compensation (this concept will be explained in further detail). Although many volunteers are driven by their personal values and desire to be of service, it helps if they have additional incentives because, like traditional staff members, on-site volunteers will face the trials and obstacles inherent in all businesses and organizations.

Recruitment

A solid volunteer program can help an organization increase the size of its staff without increasing its payroll. Vacant (or desired) positions can be filled by on-site volunteer personnel. These volunteer staff members contribute more to the organization than typical volunteer "helpers" and function like traditional employees. A one-person development office can easily create five or more full-time-equivalent on-site positions with individuals who can assist in development tasks from managing databases and compiling campaign results to overseeing direct mail appeals and thanking donors.

Most organizations are accustomed to on-site volunteers working on program-related projects. For example, a food pantry uses volunteers to sort groceries, or an advocacy organization relies on volunteers to address and stuff envelopes. Often our stereotype of these volunteers is the senior citizen looking for interesting daily activities or the Boy Scout completing community service hours to earn a merit badge. Although people who fall within these demographic groups may provide an organization with indispensable support, volunteer staff may also be recruited through many other avenues.

For example, the Urban League sponsors a national Seniors in Community Service program that assists senior workers (ages fifty-five plus) who are entering or reentering the workforce. The program has two goals: to provide seniors with the opportunity to get updated work experience and training and to supplement income and benefits for low-income program participants. Participants in this federally funded program are paid an hourly wage by the Urban League for the hours they "work" at a nonprofit organization. These seniors are dependable and wonderful at donor relations—making thank you calls, sending acknowledgment letters, staffing phone lines—time-consuming tasks that are critical to development efforts.

College and high school interns are another source of volunteer staff. Most colleges and an increasing number of high schools allow students the opportunity to work for credit instead of taking a traditional class. Internships usually last for a semester and students usually work ten to twelve hours a week. As a rule, these students are juniors or seniors. They make great volunteer staff members because, of course, their final grade depends on the quality of their work and attendance.

Establishing a good internship program takes planning, but the rewards can be worth the effort. Creativity plays a vital role in developing the internship description. It is important to consider all the development functions and match them to the expertise of the volunteer staff person. An accounting major may be interested in logging donations into the database during a direct mail campaign. A journalism student might write articles for the newsletter while a graphic design student might handle the layout and seek bids from printers. A business major may prepare agendas and compile minutes for committee and board meetings. Added benefits provided by student interns are that they often have knowledge

of the latest computer technology and programs as well as a fresh-
ness that allows them to think "outside of the box" easily. If management is open-minded, the organization can reap the rewards of
an intern's ingenuity.

Federal work-study programs are another viable resource for
recruiting college students. Through participating colleges and universities, nonprofit organizations are able to "hire" income-eligible
students as part of the students' college financial aid package. This
program currently requires a 25 percent match. For example, a student who earns $6.00 an hour would receive $4.50 of it from federal program funds and $1.50 from the sponsoring organization.
Thus, a $60.00 weekly investment would support one full-time-
equivalent staff member. These students usually have limited formal work experience but are good data entry clerks, research
assistants, typists, and receptionists.

School districts, publicly financed job training initiatives, privately funded school-to-work programs, and a host of social service agencies are all additional sources to contact for potential
volunteer staff. Use your imagination and knowledge of local programs in your area to form a partnership that provides workers on-
the-job training and real work experience. However, do not blindly
solicit volunteers. Before recruiting volunteer staff, accurately identify personnel needs and create complete job descriptions.

Begin by filling in the blank in this statement: "I could be more
efficient in my job if I could delegate the task of. . . ." The answer
might be typing general correspondence and answering phones.
Then ask further questions. How much work like this is there to do?
How much time (hours a day or a week) is needed? What expectations and standards should be placed on this position? What skills
are needed to complete this task or these tasks successfully? If the
task or tasks are specific to the organization, how much training will
be necessary? Does the organization have adequate space, equipment, or supplies to accommodate this additional worker? Are there
any concerns about or potential obstacles in creating this position?

After completing this exercise, a rudimentary job description
should emerge. Give the position a nice title (something simple but

attractive-sounding), then polish it by adding more details about the position's duties, responsibilities, and work hours, along with desired skills and abilities.

Selection

As candidates are referred to the organization, have an information packet ready to send to inquirers. In addition to a copy of the job description, the packet should include an organizational history, brochure, newsletter, or other promotional materials. Well-presented and helpful information will attract the best people to your organization. Finally, request that candidates apply formally and use a selection process, just as if they were applying for a paid position.

Orientation

Once accepted for a position, volunteer staff should be given a thorough orientation. Use this time to assure all volunteers that they are doing something valuable for themselves as well as providing a service to their community. Provide a staff handbook that outlines traditional protocol on punctuality, dress codes, disciplinary and grievance policies, emergency procedures, and so on. A handbook not only provides useful information but also helps solidify the volunteers' commitment to the organization.

On-the-job training

Training is the most important element in a volunteer staff program. It is critical to remember that some volunteers have little previous work experience. The executive or development director must be prepared to provide mentoring, set standards for the work ethic, and give specific work and skills training. Still, keep in mind that these people will probably not become long-term members of your development team. A balance must be found; the volunteer staff must be provided with the level of support necessary to help them make enough significant contributions to offset the time and energy invested in recruitment and training.

The bulk of a volunteer's training will be informal. However, despite all of their other responsibilities, executive or development directors must take care to schedule time with volunteer staff—particularly when volunteers are new and unfamiliar with the organization and their work duties. This is the time when volunteers will need the most direct supervision. It is recommended that the trainer spend as much uninterrupted time as possible with a new trainee during his or her first week and then gradually let the volunteer make the transition to minimal direct supervision.

Keep in mind that abandoned volunteers will soon become frustrated, feel unappreciated, and lose commitment. This scenario can be avoided if a method by which the volunteer can get answers to questions and receive feedback is developed and implemented. The trainer may need to set daily or weekly (depending on the volunteer's schedule or number of hours worked) one-on-one informal discussions in addition to making a point of "checking in" with volunteer staff whenever possible. Volunteers should be encouraged to write down or leave a voicemail message about any concerns that arise during times when the executive or development director is unavailable—and should receive a response quickly to prevent them from feeling petty or insignificant. As the volunteer staff grows, it will be helpful to groom a lead volunteer whose primary responsibility is to oversee and manage the activities of the volunteer staff.

Presentations and seminars

These in-house sessions should be general in nature and cover all aspects of the organization. They can be easily facilitated by a qualified volunteer staff member or guest lecturer. Their purpose is essential in making volunteers' work experience richer by helping them to understand more of its context. For example, a neighborhood community center may present information on the outcomes of local crime prevention efforts.

Team briefings

Depending on your organization's size and activities, briefings can be conducted every week or two weeks or every month. Usually these meetings last about a half-hour and are used to inform staff of current plans and objectives.

A briefing covers four major areas:

- Achievements made since the last briefing
- New initiatives under development
- Staff changes
- General housekeeping and reminders

Briefings serve two important purposes. First, they keep volunteer staff connected to the organization and feeling valued. Second, they provide a vehicle to keep every staff member up to date and the operation running smoothly.

Note that, as stated earlier, "volunteer" may not be the most appropriate description for these staff members, but the term serves to distinguish them from paid staff in the organization's budget. Remember to treat volunteer staff as you would paid staff members, and expect the same level of commitment from them. Include them in staff meetings and planning sessions. Provide designated work areas, equipment, and supplies. Develop evaluation, feedback, and staff recognition programs. Most important, thank them well . . . and often.

Working committees: Improving the quality of development-related projects

Ad hoc committees are not a new phenomenon in the nonprofit world. These committees are usually formed to assist with fundraising campaigns (advisory board), provide guidance to staff on specific operations (task force), or assist with special events (steering committee). However, establishing a "working" committee to develop, produce, and implement fundraising-related projects is a seldom-used strategy that can dramatically boost the potential of a lean development office.

Working committees are made up of specialists in a particular field who agree collectively to manage a project that cannot be absorbed by an already-taxed staff. For example, a small nonprofit invites five local public relations professionals to participate on a public relations or marketing committee that will be responsible for producing the organization's annual mail campaign. Initially, the committee will meet with staff to determine the project's goals, time lines, budget, and evaluation methods. Then the committee itself will decide how often to meet and delegate individual tasks and responsibilities to its members, including researching and writing, obtaining photographs, securing a graphic designer, soliciting and reviewing bids from printers, and so on. After these preliminary steps, the chairperson will prepare a time-and-task chart that allows the organization to monitor the committee's productivity.

The organization should support the committee by preparing agendas and minutes, sending meeting reminder notices, providing space and refreshments for meetings, and so on. A dedicated committee with a strong chairperson can be a blessing; however, be careful and intervene immediately if faced with an ineffective committee that becomes stress-producing and counterproductive by missing deadlines, producing subquality work—or no work at all.

Again, it is helpful to be creative in determining what projects could be effectively delegated to a working committee. Project ideas include producing newsletters, organizing donor recognition events or benefit functions, devising and implementing a public relations plan, or conducting program evaluations.

Board members: Developing the potential of the principal development partners

When an organization has a full complement of fundraising volunteers capable of handling the daily tasks in the development office, it can work on donor prospecting, acquisition, and relationship management—the development activities performed by the executive or development director and an active board of directors. Often, small nonprofits are managed by a board of directors that may not be accustomed to or knowledgeable in fundraising methods. Often, board meetings become so bogged down in program planning that the issue of fundraising is rarely discussed, and then only in crisis situations. Contrary to popular belief, it isn't necessary for all board members to be wealthy or have ties to major foundations. It is necessary, however, for all board members to participate in the development effort. Having clear and reasonable expectations along with accountability from peers helps solidify the directors' commitment and involvement. This is another area in which the development director as facilitator or trainer can help the organization evolve and grow.

One method to promote active board participation is to make fund development a topic at every board meeting. The donor acquisition process described in this section enables board members to enhance their fundraising efforts effectively. In this model, directors are responsible for submitting the names and complete contact information of prescreened, potential donors to the organization. As a result, board members share the responsibility of researching and screening prospects—a task that often rests solely with staff.

If the organization's board meetings are scheduled on a monthly basis, each member can generally submit the name of one new prospect at each meeting. Boards that meet less often should consider securing three or four prospects for each meeting. In either situation, the referred prospects become the respective board member's "case." Although staff usually handle any correspondence, meeting arrangements, and so on, the board member is responsible for personally contacting the prospect by phone, scheduling an on-site visit, and making any follow-up calls. Most importantly, board members report the progress and status of each "open case" (a prospect that has not yet given a contribution) at the following meeting. A typical case may proceed as follows:

February. Ms. Active Member submits the name and address of Mr. Caring Citizen, who has a local family foundation. Ms. Active Member provides a brief review of the foundation's funding history, application procedures, and so on.

March. Ms. Active Member reports that an introductory letter was mailed to Mr. Caring Citizen following the last board meeting and that an on-site visit was held last week. Mr. Citizen seemed very interested in the organization's cause and stated that a request letter could be sent to his foundation for consideration ($5,000). Ms. Member also submits the name of Mr. Local Entrepreneur as a new prospect.

April. Ms. Active Member reports that she contacted Mr. Caring Citizen to follow up on the request letter. It was received and a decision will be made next month. As for Mr. Entrepreneur, he was mailed an introductory letter. He has not responded to any messages left by Ms. Member. Ms. Member also submits the XYZ Corporation Foundation as a new prospect.

May. Ms. Active Member reports that a $2,500 contribution was received from the Citizen Family Foundation. An acknowledgment letter was sent and a personal thank you call made by Ms. Member. Mr. Entrepreneur did not agree to a site visit but said to keep him informed of the organization's activities. And, finally, a grant proposal for the XYZ Corporation Foundation is due on the twenty-fifth of this month. The foundation does not entertain site visits until the proposal has been reviewed and accepted by its board for consideration.

The exact entries listed would be noted by the board secretary in a "prospect binder" (a simple three-ring binder tabbed by board members' names followed by individual pages for each case). This system helps to monitor the prospect's status and ensures that the prospect is contacted on a regular basis by a board or staff member.

Soliciting a new prospect will result in one of three outcomes. The prospect is either *completed* (makes a donation and therefore needs and deserves ongoing communication with the organization), *open* (expresses interest in the organization and requires continuing relationship building), or *dead* (after many attempts at relationship-building, the prospect continues to show no interest or propensity to support the organization).

If there is no response to repeated requests for donations, a prospect should be "transferred" to another board member. Sometimes one individual's approach can influence or deter a prospective donor. The transfer also allows the prospect to develop another link to the organization while the nonprofit gains an additional perspective on the prospect. If there continues to be disinterest, after careful consideration and recommendation by the board as a whole the prospect can be removed from the process.

A director's term is usually for three years. Therefore, this method inherently raises questions about a board member's responsibility and activities during years two and three of the program. Using the example of a board that meets monthly (with a three-month summer break), a director would submit nine new prospects per fiscal year for a maximum of twenty-seven prospects during a member's first term.

When a board member has accumulated twenty cases (which takes over two years), he or she should suspend actively researching additional prospects. The reasoning behind this strategy is that new and prospective donors should be treated like newlyweds—part of an intimate relationship full of mutual respect, caring, support, and encouragement. If board members manage more than twenty cases, it is likely that some donors will not receive what they need from the relationship.

In addition, staff must actively monitor and participate in the donor acquisition process—particularly during times of board transition. As directors rotate off the board, staff members can maintain the organization's relationship with donors. When a change occurs, it is the staff's responsibility to make certain that there is a smooth transition to a freshman or other board member.

This prospecting method identifies and manages many critical development activities. First, it assures that prospects are not lost. Second, the process helps board members stay focused and actively involved in the organization's fundraising efforts while providing a framework to assist them in making contact with potential donors. The system also offers a mechanism in which directors are accountable to their peers and encourages healthy competition and camaraderie among fellow board members.

Conclusion

In this do-more-with-less era, take caution not to underestimate the planning and commitment necessary to implement a development-driven volunteer program. The organization's board of directors should provide governance that places realistic expectations on staff and their limited resources. The examples in this chapter are by no means quick fixes for a lean staff.

Lack of adequate preparation by staff is the primary cause of an ineffective or counterproductive development-driven volunteer program. The development professional heading the program must be well-organized and patient, consistent yet flexible. To establish and sustain a successful program, the staff will devote significant time to the tasks outlined earlier—recruiting and selecting volunteers; facilitating individual and group training sessions; developing work plans; monitoring individual, committee, and board productivity; and providing mediation, support, motivation, and feedback to volunteer staff—while maintaining strict fiscal controls and ensuring good stewardship of contribution dollars.

Successfully managing these tasks while demonstrating sound planning, reasonable objectives, and diligence will result in staff, directors, and community partners who collectively augment the organization's fundraising capacity.

MARISSA C. WEAVER *is the executive director of America's Black Holocaust Museum, Milwaukee, and runs a one-person development office using many of the techniques described here. She also serves on the board of directors of the National Society of Fundraising Executives, Milwaukee chapter.*

A longtime community activist offers a personal recollection of the volunteer experience.

4

Lessons from a professional volunteer

Barbara A. Stein

THERE IS a first time for everything in the nonprofit arena—a first board meeting, a first leadership position, a first capital campaign. And there is a first time for writing for a professional journal about those experiences. Although I've attended hundreds of board meetings, held several dozen leadership positions, and led a number of capital campaigns, nothing is as anxiety-producing as writing about such activities for a journal that is destined to be read by professionals. But guts and grit got me through many volunteer challenges, and I've stuck with this one.

Invest time in volunteers for significant dividends

Great! You stuck with me instead of turning to the next chapter! And take it from me—sticking with people is what all volunteers need, no matter their level of participation or experience. My own experience tells me that even though I have a forty-year volunteer career behind me, I still feel like a neophyte when it comes to a new organization or a new position in an old organization. It is critically important for a nonprofit professional or a volunteer in a leadership slot to assist, advise, and encourage newcomers no matter how

NEW DIRECTIONS FOR PHILANTHROPIC FUNDRAISING, NO. 20, SUMMER 1998 © JOSSEY-BASS PUBLISHERS

much experience they may have. I believe that organizations lose a significant percentage of their volunteer participation because individuals feel awkward, uninformed, or neglected. The idea of assigning a mentor or buddy to each rookie is a sound one, both for the beginner and for the veteran. When partnered, the veteran feels needed and responsible; the fledgling feels protected and valued.

Case in point. When I was pregnant with my second son, I was held hostage by my three-year-old and my inability to drive. I needed a creative outlet and I needed one fast! While eagerly devouring a newsletter from a childbirth association, I discovered that the group was looking for an editor. I called and volunteered for the job. I was told I could do anything I wanted and just to be sure to meet the publishing deadline. From that point forward, I neither saw nor heard from the organization's leadership again. I conducted interviews over the phone, I read professional pamphlets, and I translated the information into everyday language for the harried housewife. I thought I was terrific. *I was published.*

I was ignored. No one ever called to comment or compliment. Suffice it to say that I used the arrival of my second son as an excuse to discontinue my activities. One friendly nudge by someone, anyone, would have brought me back to the typewriter. No one nudged; I didn't budge. This is a classic example of how *not* to treat a volunteer.

Fast forward a decade or so, and I'm engaged in creating and presenting an educational forum for a Hadassah Health Conference. As we all do when pressed for time and a new approach, I pull out some old material from the childbirth association newsletter file. After putting together a perfectly brilliant presentation, I run my ideas past the former conference chair who has been wonderfully "user friendly."

This blessed woman had provided me with her event files, answered questions, and was "on call." Thus, I felt completely comfortable in asking her to review my final plan. She read my material, she smiled and nodded—I was happy. Then a subtle change came over her face. One eye closed. Her breathing pattern changed. Ever so slowly she looked up and quietly asked if I understood that the audience would be made up of Jewish women from the three major areas of Judaism: reform, conservative, and ortho-dox. And since orthodox women always dress modestly, cover their heads, and never wear sleeveless outfits or short skirts, it might be a tad indelicate to discuss openly the more intimate details of nat-ural childbirth. She carefully pointed out that what might be per-fectly appropriate to "reveal" in one organization was not quite as appropriate in another forum with certain women present. Bless that woman, she saved me a lot of embarrassment and prevented some orthodox ladies in the audience from having a coronary!

Lesson learned. Take the time to interact personally with the vol-unteer who is assuming a new position, or encourage the volunteer who is passing on a portfolio to meet with her successor. This face-to-face meeting offers a number of benefits. First, the professional gets a sense of the volunteer's level of commitment and expertise. Second, both parties share expectations about deadlines, duties, and dependability. Third, an in-person meeting cements a relationship, and when it comes to interactions between professional and vol-unteer, a good relationship is all there is. And finally, keep in mind that a volunteer does not work for *pay*, but really appreciates the *payback* of a job well done.

Be wary of "founder's syndrome"

At the beginning of my volunteer career, I was always the new kid on the block. Everyone knew more than I did. Everyone had "been there, done that." For the most part, the folks sitting on the board of directors were veteran supporters of the organization—they owned it. In some cases they were founding members, in other instances their grandmother had gone to grade school with the first president of the board . . . and don't you forget it. Business was to be conducted in a certain way and woe to the newcomer who sug-gested changing the status quo. Attempting to alter long-standing practices was a deadly experience for an enthusiastic novice. I can-not count the times I heard the phrase, "But we've always done it that way," or "We already tried that and it didn't work!" These statements and the attitude they represent often causes the marginally committed volunteer to look elsewhere for a more friendly group that is willing to support creativity. But if an organization's mission has the capacity to attract a new generation of supporters, it is incumbent on veteran members to act as a bridge from the past to the future.

Case in point. Joining one organization that had just celebrated its eighty-fifth year of community service in Milwaukee, I noted that there were nine former presidents serving on the board of directors. This can be a blessing; this can be a curse. In this case, the blessing was that the former leadership still had a strong interest in the welfare of the group. The curse was that the leaders subtly discouraged innovative programs that might shift the limelight from past accomplishments. I was of the opinion that if a new community service project was not launched soon, a significant number of new, younger members would look elsewhere to invest their precious few volunteer hours. I was in a quandary. I came to the realization that this battle was not mine to fight alone. I needed an ally.

I sought out the past president I believed to be the most reasonable and laid out my vision for a meaningful community service project that would bring renewed public acclaim to the organization. My goal was to involve a group of younger women who would eventually step up to leadership positions and thus ensure that the organization would survive and thrive. And I asked for one favor: Would she act as an adviser to the project and present the idea at the next board meeting? I then asked three young, bright, and enthusiastic proponents of the project to be there as well to lend their support to the veteran member. Dear Dorothy proposed the idea for the new program with a reminder that it was the logical next step for an organization that had brilliantly developed noteworthy pilots in the past. With the three younger members' insightful comments and their pledge to work with the veteran leaders to launch the project, the program was unanimously endorsed. Mission accomplished. There was no battle, everyone came out a winner.

Lesson learned. There is nothing as past as a past president who doesn't recognize that she is no longer the standard-bearer of the organization. However, respect is definitely due those loyal veterans who did not abandon the group following their leadership term. It is also imperative that members working their way up in the ranks of an organization make certain to recognize and utilize the wisdom of the veteran members. When organizations make major changes in order to remain viable, it is incumbent on the reformers to be sensitive to history and the members who made that history.

Nevertheless, activists must make a commitment to growth and development. Savvy change makers in several of my organizations have established presidents' councils, which cater to the needs and egos of past leaders while still keeping them involved but away from the business of running the group. The former presidents plan their own meetings, agendas, and social gatherings. Council members are invited on an annual basis to present a historical minute at a meeting of the "junior group." They are invited to the annual meeting and all fundraising events of the organization and are appropriately recognized for their past contributions. What is most amusing to me today is that I am a member of three presidents' councils myself and am looked upon with affection and benevolence by those young whippersnappers who currently lead the organization. What do they know anyway? Why, in my day. . . .

Hold people accountable

Organizations depend on an active board of directors to work toward achieving the mission of the group. The board is charged with making and monitoring policies, raising funds, and encouraging participation and new leadership. If volunteer board members don't do their job, the organization does not flourish. The simple fact is that board members *must* attend meetings and take the job of directing the organization seriously. Absent board and committee members do a great disservice to the cause. I have observed heretofore active and effective board and committee members slacking off because less productive volunteers are not held accountable by fellow members or paid professionals. By looking the other way when a volunteer fails to perform, they jeopardize the viability of the organization by tacitly condoning poor performance. Poor performance can wreck a project and discourage active volunteers. But what do you do with chronically absent board or committee members? You can't fine them. You can't stare them down when they do make an appearance. You must take immediate steps to deal with them, and you must do so in a nonconfrontational manner.

Case in point. As the president of one organization, I was asked to speak with a founding member who hadn't been attending meetings. I was petrified! How do you fire a founder? After complimenting her on her foresight in establishing our group, I went on to call attention to how far we had come. I then pointed out how critically important each and every board member was to the success of the group and how much time each had spent at meetings. Just before I launched into the fatal blow, she interrupted me and said she felt that under the circumstances she could no longer devote the time that the group genuinely warranted. She felt her slot should be filled by someone willing to help the organization take the next steps toward accomplishing its goals. She was gracious. She stepped down. I was grateful. I was exhausted!

One effective tool I have used to keep board or committee members on track and productive is to assign a veteran member to each newcomer. The veteran is advised to call the novice before each meeting and then sit with the member at the meetings. They are often paired on committees. Before long, the partners have bonded and neither will disappoint the other by not showing up without an explanation. I have also made it a point to schedule a once-a-year meeting with the novice board member to find out his or her impressions and suggestions on how to lead the organization better.

Lesson learned. The traditional camp "buddy system" not only applies when going into the deep end of the pool but also works quite well when building effective board participation. If operating systems break down and projects go haywire, the problems can often be traced to ineffective interaction on the part of staff, leadership, or buddy. Staff or elected leaders must immediately intervene to get the ball rolling again. If issues are not addressed, if projects are not put back on track, if volunteers don't complete their assigned task, then the message is clear: the issue wasn't important, the project wasn't necessary, the task wasn't that important. Apathy is the silent enemy of many organizations.

Make fundraising number one for everyone

I think that our calling most charitable organizations *nonprofits* is really rather strange since 50 percent of our task in the group is to raise funds—or "make a profit"—which we reinvest in the organization. Each and every volunteer committee and board member must face the fact that fundraising is of prime importance and, therefore, everyone is a fundraiser. Every organization I've worked with constantly emphasized the need to expand its donor base. We courted corporations and ferreted out foundations. We sought government grants and romanced known philanthropists. There was a never-ending search for the diminishing dollar.

Grassroots groups have a more difficult time because they are competing with larger and more visible institutions and agencies. However, no matter what the nonprofit's budget is, volunteers are a critical element in effective fundraising. The well-established organizations have experienced fund development staffs that are able to mobilize volunteer board members effectively to assist their efforts. Much of my early involvement with fundraising was at the grassroots level and it was there that I witnessed or participated in some of the most creative and successful fundraising events or campaigns.

Case in point. At the age of fourteen I was elected fundraising chair of my chapter of the B'nai B'rith, a group of Jewish teenage girls. Other chapters were selling chocolate-covered matzos, Chanukah wrapping paper, and the like. I thought long and hard and tried to be creative. I came up with what I thought was a unique product and convinced the gals that this item would bring in oodles of funds. I was right. No other group of Jewish girls in the entire city went door-to-door selling Christmas tree ornaments! Being an alert teenager, I had figured out that in order to be financially successful we needed to tap a whole new market and that there were "a lot more of them out there than there were of us." We created quite a stir, but we sold case upon case of ornaments. We made a bundle!

Lesson learned. Encouraging volunteers to be creative, take a risk, and do the unexpected can be the key to a successful fund drive or special event. Traditional fundraising campaigns can be effective, but it is often the clever theme that catches the attention of a potential donor and captures the heart of a hardworking volunteer. Whatever the campaign or special event vehicle used to generate funds, volunteer input is critical. Planning and pizzazz can be potent partners in organizational fundraising.

Use the volunteer connection effectively

Volunteers form an amazing network within the community and use it liberally to spread the organizational message. Once convinced that an organization's mission is worthy of their time, energy, and financial support, astute volunteers tap into their spheres of influence and enlist the aid of family, friends, and colleagues. If they are successful salespeople, they not only raise additional funds for the cause but also assist in developing future fundraisers. Savvy volunteers rarely miss an opportunity to stump the financial hustings to uncover hidden resources.

Case in point. Having lost track of an organizational buddy over the years, I was pleased to reconnect and exchange pleasantries. She inquired about my current activities and I mentioned my involvement with the Task Force on Family Violence of Milwaukee. She expressed interest and asked if we could get together so she could learn more about the issue. On our appointed visit, I brought materials about three domestic violence service agencies and touted each as commendable. Nine months passed before I heard from her again, this time at second hand. Within the space of two hours I received three wildly enthusiastic phone calls from three very happy executive directors; they had just received letters and checks from a family foundation stating that because of the information I had shared with my friend they were each recipients of a grant for $25,000! Who knew?!

Lesson learned. Don't underestimate the value of friendship and networking. I truly had no clue that my long-lost friend directed her family foundation's assets or that my presentation to her had been so effective. I really cared about the movement and I gladly shared my passion with an old friend.

Forty years of volunteering at a glance

Over my volunteer career I have had the opportunity to work with a wide variety of organizations and agencies. I have conferred with dozens of executive directors, planned hundreds of membership and fundraising campaigns, and staged countless events that have attracted thousands of folks. Each activity has presented its own set of challenges and rewards. It goes without saying that the size and scope of a particular nonprofit organization determines the level of volunteer involvement.

In grassroots groups where there is no professional staff, volunteer input keeps the organization viable. Members meet in homes and use "the good offices" of family and friends to underwrite or cut the cost of secretarial tasks, copying, and mailings. The percentage of profit returned on dollars invested is enormous, as is the satisfaction level of the enthusiastic volunteers. Many folks will only volunteer with such groups and proudly trace membership in the organization back several generations. I first learned the ropes in such groups and I have great respect for them. These grassroots groups fired my passion for good causes, gave me an opportunity to develop various skills, and prepared me to take the next step in my volunteer adventures.

When I was invited to "move up" and serve on the board of organizations that employed executive directors and support staff, I thought I had died and gone to heaven. No more sorting third-class mailings, no more taking minutes at meetings and spending hours on the phone setting up meetings. But to my surprise, I missed the day-to-day contact with my fellow volunteers who shared the same vision and passion. Strategic planning was more focused but less compelling. Fundraising was more efficient and membership details were more accurate, but the faces behind the names were not as familiar. Fellow board members had more experience and skills to share, but personal interaction outside the meetings was minimal. I enjoyed being directed and supported, but I missed being in charge.

As I moved into leadership positions with organizations running multimillion dollar campaigns, I was struck by the number of wealthy donors I had never known existed. These new volunteer contacts thankfully translated into substantial amounts of money raised and allocated to worthy causes. The vast professional staffs were well-trained and available to volunteers. Although they were more influential and felt prestigious, the big boards could never capture the intimacy and urgency of the grassroots groups. All in all, it was not a bad trade-off. Bottom line—a good cause is a good cause.

Having volunteered with many organizations, I have found strengths and weaknesses in each. Every organization has given me invaluable experiences and afforded me opportunities that I never would have had if I had not chosen to volunteer. Forty years of community service has taught me that volunteering can be rewarding and challenging. Volunteering enabled me to write my own ticket as far as what path I wished to pursue and with whom I wished to pursue it. Although I have never been paid a salary for my efforts, I have definitely received great benefits!

BARBARA A. STEIN *is a respected and dedicated volunteer and philan-thropist in the Milwaukee community. She currently serves on a number of boards and is in the leadership of United Way of Greater Milwaukee.*

Most organizations agree that they have a moral imperative to reflect in their makeup the diversity of the communities they serve. This chapter describes how organizations can strengthen the funding base and raise more money by bringing all constituencies—based on gender, race, age, sexual orientation, disability, and so on—into fundraising.

5

Building a fundraising base that reflects the cultural diversity of the organization

Kim Klein

MANY YEARS AGO when I was living in Brooklyn, New York, I was asked to do a fundraising training for a very interesting coalition that had formed in the wake of a beating of a Korean merchant. The alleged attackers were Haitians, who were responding to the accusation by the merchant that he had caught a Haitian woman shoplifting. The actual truth about that incident never became known, but in the days that followed it a great deal of anger and hostility was vented both verbally and physically. Residents of primarily Caribbean neighborhoods accused Korean merchants operating there of price-gouging, never hiring local people to work in their stores, and controlling businesses in neighborhoods they did not live in. In turn, many of the merchants accused the

NEW DIRECTIONS FOR PHILANTHROPIC FUNDRAISING, NO. 20, SUMMER 1998 © JOSSEY-BASS PUBLISHERS

neighborhood residents of thievery, vandalism, and unwillingness to work. Within this welter of race and class dynamics, cultural misunderstanding and frustration, a small group of people decided to try to diffuse the anger and violence.

A Korean minister and two Haitian neighborhood activists called a meeting. The strategy of the group was simple: get people talking with each other. Through church exchanges, going into schools, and organizing town meetings, it was hoped that a lot of frustration would naturally dissolve as people understood each other better. None of the organizers thought this would solve the problems, but they all felt it couldn't hurt.

Several meetings later, I was asked to help develop a fundraising strategy. During the first part of the meeting, I was told, we would review work that had been done by various committees; then the group would break up into committees. I would meet with the fundraising committee.

About twenty-five people attended the meeting I went to. Of the twenty-five, eight were from Haiti or Jamaica. Five were African Americans, seven were Korean—including three merchants—and the remaining five were white, of Italian or Irish descent. Thirteen of us had been born in the United States, including four of the white participants.

The meeting proceeded smoothly, and then the chair called for us to break into committees. He introduced me as a fundraising expert and asked the fundraising committee to meet in Room One, down the hall. I walked there and waited for the fundraising committee to join me. I was taken aback when the only people who came into the room were all the white people. I asked how the committees had been chosen, and a woman said that the chair had made the assignments. She.went on to say that since she had been in the United States for only a few months (she was from Italy), she really knew nothing about fundraising and had never done anything like it in her country. She thought she might have been better on the education committee, because she was a schoolteacher. After some discussion of how much money needed to be raised ($10,000), in what time period (over the next six months of the school year), and for what (books, videos, and speaker fees), three others of those present chimed in that they had never done any fundraising either. I decided to find the coalition chair.

I asked him if we could reconvene the whole group and ask for volunteers to be on the committee. Raising a small amount of money for a short-term project like this seemed a good opportunity to use fundraising also to further the goals of the group. I envisioned some block parties, some door-to-door canvassing inside some of the big apartment buildings, and possibly a raffle to involve merchants in donating prizes and selling tickets. The coalition chair called the group back together. I explained what I had in mind and asked for volunteers. One person from the original committee raised her hand, followed by one Haitian, two African Americans, and the chair himself, who was Korean. He then asked if anyone else wanted to switch committees. There was minimal shuffling—the original fundraising committee fanned out among education, relations with police, and church outreach. We went back to the meeting. I now had people on the committee who had done a lot of fundraising. My suggestions were rejected in favor of two events, which ultimately raised over $13,000. The first was a barbecue contest. You paid $5 to enter your barbecue and you had to bring enough food to feed fifty people. You paid $15 to eat. Because barbecue is a favorite food of all the ethnic groups involved, it was a great event. People brought all kinds of food and set up booths. It was a multiblock party that lasted all afternoon and into the late evening. The second event was a second collection at a number of churches.

This group was more dramatic than many (because it was so diverse to begin with), but the tendency to see fundraising as the prerogative or talent or job of a certain group of people—usually defined by race, age, and class—is not uncommon. The previously described organization defined it by race. Sometimes the assumption is not that a certain group cannot do fundraising but rather that those individuals would be good at a certain kind of fundraising. For example, people under twenty-five are often given the task of organizing a special event or selling a product to make money.

Wealthy people are always thought to be better at face-to-face solicitation, even though having money does not give anyone skill in raising it. Requests for planned giving are often directed at older people, even though none of us knows when we are going to die and some planned giving strategies can benefit a wider age margin than is often realized.

Why cultural diversity deserves attention in fundraising

There are two reasons to pay attention to cultural diversity when planning for fundraising. First, the world and the United States as one country in the world are culturally diverse. Second, organizations will raise more money if they take these facts into account in planning for fundraising.

Reason 1: The world and the United States are culturally diverse

I work almost entirely with organizations that are defined as "out of the mainstream." These organizations work on a broad span of issues, from public education, accessible mass transit, and rent control to health, peace, the environment, foreign policy, and so on. That these issues are considered out of the mainstream has led many of us to ask, "Where is the mainstream, anyway?" The organizations cover the gamut of civil rights issues, including those of the poor, the physically or mentally challenged, gays and lesbians, seniors, youth, women, and people of color. Indeed, sharp-eyed readers will have noticed something about the people on this list: they are the majority of people. Most people in the world are people of color; in several states, including the one I live in, so-called minorities make up the majority of the population. More than half the people in the world are women. And the majority of the world's population lives in poverty. What we call the "third world" would be more appropriately called the "majority world."

Even in cities and towns that are racially homogeneous there are vast age spreads; there are also cultural differences between neighborhoods, there are gay people and straight people, and so on. The point is obvious: to be a viable nonprofit with more than a handful of members requires attracting people of all types, because that's how the world is. For many of us, understanding this requires a shift in what we think of (often involuntarily) as the norm. For example, a wonderful board member of a group I work with recently made this announcement: "We have recruited four new board members— one is a woman and one is Asian." Another board member said, "What are the other two, chopped liver?" This remark made people realize how unconsciously we think about people: the norm is white, straight, and male, and everyone is defined against that norm. As another board member pointed out, "You probably wouldn't announce that you had four new board members and two of them were white men." Assumptions about who the norm represents are pervasive. School curricula make note of *authors* and *black authors*. A newspaper headline recently announced a conference for journalists, with a special panel of "disabled journalists."

Reason 2: Organizations will raise more money if they take these facts into account

By shifting our core assumptions about the world, we will raise more money! If the majority of us are, demographically, actually members of various minority groups, then we will want to tailor our message accordingly. The evidence about who gives away money follows closely the pattern of who makes up the majority of people. For example, of the three nongovernment sources of funding—individuals, foundations, and corporations—individuals give away the lion's share. For all the time during which we have been keeping records—now over sixty years—85 to 90 percent of the money given away is given by individuals. Only about 10 to 12 percent of funding comes from foundations and corporations and, of course, the source of most foundation assets is the accumulated wealth of an individual or family. Seven out of ten adults give away money. When we look closely at which people give away all this money—almost $135 billion in 1996—we see that about 83 percent of it came from households with annual incomes under

$59,000. We see that donors are fairly evenly divided by education, with the majority (37 percent) being high school graduates, 22 percent having some college, and 25 percent being college graduates. The remaining 15 percent have less than a high school education. Fifty-four percent are employed full time, 11 percent part time, and 34 percent are unemployed. Slightly more women than men make contributions, and givers tend to cross all racial lines (American Association of Fund-Raising Counsel, 1997; Hodgkinson, Weitzman, Noga, and Gorski, 1992).

Cases in point

Let's examine what fundraising looks like in organizations that plan around whatever diversity is present in their board, staff, volunteers, and constituencies. Let's look at some examples and then pull out the lessons to be learned.

An Oakland, California, group organizes on issues of police accountability, lead paint in schools, and toxic dumping: all issues affecting poor neighborhoods in the city. Every year the group has a fundraising dinner. The members of the organization make the food, and people pay $15 a ticket to get in. More than fifty people work on the dinner every year. Because the membership is very multicultural, the food always includes barbecued ribs, potato salad, roasted chicken, egg rolls, tamales, rice and beans, lasagna, and several kinds of desserts. The organization's members put together an adbook for the dinner and sell ads to merchants in the neighborhoods in which they work, but they also sell to other nonprofits, unions, and a wide circle of friends who have started coming to the dinners because of the food. With the admission fees paid by the two hundred to three hundred people attending the dinner and the proceeds from the adbook, this group nets anywhere from $5,000 to $10,000.

A program for battered women in a rural community started a major donor program by creating categories of donors based on things people had in common. To be a major donor you had to make a gift of $100, and then you were invited to join various "clubs." Some of the clubs were Local Merchants, Vacation Homeowners, Hiking Club, Gardeners' Club, Retirees' Club (this one had some of the same members as Vacation Homeowners), Anglers, High School Jocks, and Odd Ducks. The latter was a group of self-identified writers, artists, musicians, and others who felt they didn't fit in anywhere else. To qualify as a club only three members were required, and each person got a little certificate printed up with the help of a graphics program owned by one of the Odd Ducks members. There were no other benefits for belonging to these clubs, except a certain camaraderie. Sometimes the organization invited people to get-togethers. The money was very important to the group, but so was the feeling that all kinds of people were interested in stopping violence against women.

An environmental organization working in very low income and primarily immigrant neighborhoods had a lot of trouble getting its membership drive off the ground. Membership dues were set at $15 and although the group was able to raise money from a large number of people, almost none came from the neighborhoods the organization served. Thinking that the dues were too high, the membership committee lowered them to $10, and later to $5. Neither move helped generate more memberships. Finally, one of the members explained that the group didn't need to make the membership cheaper. Rather, what was needed was a way to pay without using a check, because few of the neighborhoods' residents had checking accounts. The organization set up a system whereby one of the members who owned a store agreed to take in the contributions and give receipts every Saturday. People brought cash and got a membership card and a receipt. Most people paid $15, and soon a high percentage of residents in the neighborhoods had joined.

A health clinic focusing on primary care and family planning that delivered more than half of its services to uninsured people conducted a phone-athon to lapsed donors and to a list of people that it thought would be interested in its work. The teenage daughter of a board member showed up to volunteer and ended up being the biggest income-generator of the evening. The coordinator asked what her secret was. She said that she and her friends had done so much fundraising in order to accomplish the things they wanted to do—including going to Cuba on a student exchange, taking their choir to New York City for a competition, and taking their Sunday school class to Greece—that she felt very comfortable asking for money. The coordinator asked if she and her friends would like to help out a second night. She volunteered, and the next evening she brought six friends. They raised more money than any other group had in the history of the clinic's phone-athons.

Lessons to be learned

Are these stories about diversity? Yes and no. They are actually about common sense, which I believe is fundamental to building a diverse fundraising base. Based on these and other stories, I will suggest some guidelines for working with cultural diversity when raising money.

Remember that there are two aspects to using cultural diversity in fundraising. The first is the people you raise money from, and the second is the people you work with to raise the money. There is clearly an interrelationship here—the more diverse the group that raises the money, the more diverse the donor base will be, and the more diverse the donor base, the more people available to help raise the money.

Watch your assumptions. After twenty-two years in fundraising, I can testify that there are two kinds of people in the world: havers and givers. As I said earlier, 70 percent of adults are givers. Givers give and havers have. Some poor people are havers. What little they have, they hang on to. Some rich people are havers, and the fact that they have more than they can spend in several lifetimes doesn't cause them to give any of it away. Givers come in all types. Some are more generous than others, but you cannot predict that based on age, education, income, gender, or any other variable. If you make it a habit to look at every person who comes through your organization as a giver, and then as a person who might be willing to help raise money, you will never overlook any possible helpers or gifts. Of course, you may be wrong, but far better to be wrong because you thought the person might give when he or she wasn't going to than to lose a gift because you assumed the person couldn't give.

Figure out what people like to do and feel comfortable doing. Few people of any cultural background feel comfortable raising money, so don't present the task as that alone. Remember my first example of the fundraising dinner in Oakland? Most people love to eat and some people love to cook. Put those together and you have the basis of an event. It can be helpful to create a list of things that are required for fundraising and ask people to fill in what they are willing to do. Such items include making phone calls, cooking for a crowd, going door-to-door in their own neighborhood or in a neighborhood where they don't know anyone, addressing envelopes, writing fundraising letters, and so on. Of course, sometimes people are not sure what they are good at or are embarrassed to volunteer for big tasks, even if they think they could do them. You may need to let people know that you have confidence in their ability to do something, or even ask them directly if they are willing to try something you think they might be good at. Sometimes people assume that to be a fundraiser they have to be well-educated or comfortable around affluence or be a salesperson. Of course these qualities are helpful, but they are not required.

Don't rush to conclusions in solving problems. The environmental group that kept lowering its dues because it assumed that the membership fee was too high did not allow for any other thing to be the problem. The real problem in this group was that no neighborhood people were on the membership committee, so the committee members were trying to figure out what to do for a group of people they knew only slightly. Once they invited two neighborhood people to join the committee, it became clear that the problem was the inability to write checks. Many people in their community do not use banks. They pay most bills in cash and the rest in postal orders. The issue was providing a way for them to pay in cash, not the amount required.

Keep careful records of what people do well, and use those in future planning. For example, the young people who were so successful in the phone-athon ought now to be invited to the major gifts committee. Their comfort level in asking for money will be useful in many ways. Keep in mind that people grow out of some strategies and into others. Many people start their fundraising efforts doing special events, and as they become more comfortable with these events, they are willing to go to other strategies. As you keep records, think about what a person has learned from a particular strategy and how that might be helpful in another. For example, creating a script for a phone-athon requires some of the same skills as writing a press release or making a pitch at a house party.

Educate your volunteer force about who really gives money and what is really true about charities. I have seen many people burst into applause and laugh with relief when they learn that the majority of money given to charities in the United States comes from individuals and that most of those people are middle class, working class, and poor. The news media gives the impression that most giving comes from corporations, wealthy people, and foundations. Grassroots groups in particular waste precious time trying to break into those worlds, trying to meet people who they only imagine exist. When they find out that in fact most money is given by ordinary people, they are thrilled. They already know all the people they need to know to raise all the money they need to raise.

Think long-term. Who is going to run the development office in five years? In ten years? Help the young people in your organization see development as a career, and if they show interest help them get experience and knowledge. There are degree tracks at universities for those people who wish to make the nonprofit sector their career. Unfortunately, these programs are not well advertised, and the nonprofit career is still not one to be found at job fairs and career-day expositions. We need to change that.

Ultimately, building a fundraising base that reflects the diversity of the organization and the community requires a constant and unflinching commitment to do so. There are struggles involved. There are bound to be misunderstandings, resentment, and confrontations. Sadly, our society is not naturally diverse. People do not fluidly cross race or age lines; women and men rarely work together as equal partners; class remains the primary stumbling block.

Sometimes commitment to diversity comes as a demand of the funders or something a group thinks it "should" do, even if it would rather not. A commitment made in order to get funding or to relieve guilt will not last long, and the results will not be satisfying. Similarly, if a group makes a sincere commitment to incorporate diversity into its fundraising program, it cannot expect immediate results. The work required may be long and sometimes tedious. The group may go around in circles as often as it makes true progress.

But groups that have made the commitment and that keep working on building diversity into their organizations and into their fundraising do find that they can raise more money and form friendships and alliances even outside of the work. Most important, they see how rich and beautifully complex life can be.

Reinhold Niebuhr, the great Protestant theologian, says this: "Nothing that is worth doing can be achieved in our lifetime; therefore we must be saved by hope. Nothing which is true or beautiful or good makes complete sense in any immediate context of history; therefore we must be saved by faith. Nothing we do, however virtuous, can be accomplished alone; therefore we are saved by love. No virtuous act is quite as virtuous from the standpoint of our friend or foe as it is from our standpoint. Therefore we must be saved by the final favor of love, which is forgiveness."

References

American Association of Fund-Raising Counsel. *Giving USA*. New York: American Association of Fund-Raising Counsel Trust for Philanthropy, 1997.

Hodgkinson, V. A., Weitzman, M. S., Noga, S. M., and Gorski, H. A. *Giving and Volunteering in the United States*. Vol. 2. Washington, D.C.: INDEPENDENT SECTOR, 1992.

KIM KLEIN *is an internationally known fundraiser and trainer. She is the owner of Chardon Press, which publishes materials that strengthen the nonprofit sector and promote social justice, the author of* Fundraising for Social Change, *and the editor and publisher of* Grassroots Fundraising Journal. *Klein has provided training and consultation in all fifty states and sixteen countries and is best known for adapting traditional fundraising techniques for use by grassroots nonprofits.*

Benefits or special events are a reality for most nonprofits. This chapter offers techniques to convert special event buyers into annual fund donors.

6

Putting the benefit back into fundraising benefits

Tracy Wayson

"THEY'RE STAFF-INTENSIVE and they burn out volunteers."

"They never generate new donors."

"Life would be so much easier without them."

You've probably heard it all. In fact, you may have uttered each of these statements when involved with a special event. Although events—also known as benefit fundraising—will never be the most effective or efficient tool for building long-term donor loyalty, they are a reality for most nonprofit organizations.

In the midst of increasing concern over the cost of raising funds to support a mission, it is crucial that organizations evaluate their event efforts and returns on an ongoing basis. New guidelines from the American Institute of Certified Public Accountants on the costs associated with raising funds have focused attention on events and present unique burdens for smaller and newer organizations (Goodman, 1998, p. 33). Traditionally, the value of a benefit has been measured by the income-minus-expense equation. This approach perpetuates the execution of events that are not integrated into the overall plan for developing donors and feeds the

NEW DIRECTIONS FOR PHILANTHROPIC FUNDRAISING, NO. 20, SUMMER 1998 © JOSSEY-BASS PUBLISHERS

criticism over fundraising expenses. Event planning with the goal of converting the special event buyer to an annual fund donor increases the value of the event and the effort involved in benefit fundraising. Now the question is, how?

Planning to turn ticket buyers into donors

If your organization has an annual campaign, chances are you have a plan to carry out the campaign. You've answered questions like these: What is the case statement? Who will be solicited? How will we communicate the message? The result is a thoughtful plan to engage individuals in the mission of the organization and thus to get a gift demonstrating their support.

Most plans for special events stop after detailing the schedule of mailing invitations, selecting a menu, and determining seating arrangements. But converting a ticket buyer into a donor also requires a deliberate plan. Identification, education, cultivation, and solicitation are cornerstones of the plan.

Identifying conversion prospects

With any fundraising strategy, it is important to qualify the potentially endless list of possible donors. Although rare, some events are so mission-specific that you can make a fair assumption that those who attend are the target. More often, however, nonprofit leaders make a *ready, fire, aim* analysis: whoever comes to our event is whom we are aiming to reach (Miller, 1996, p. 115). But it doesn't have to be feast or famine. Identification is the process of precision aiming. Aim is improved by improving the benefit invitation list in two ways.

Invite nondonors

First, if the justification for an event is the opportunity to convert, invite nondonors. Frequently, an event invitation list is limited to previous donors and the event becomes a social opportunity for current constituencies. Have a goal for the number of nondonors you would like in attendance and invite four to five individuals for every one you hope will attend. Ideally, these individuals have been singled out for their potential interest in the work of the organization. Perhaps they support a similar organization or were added to your prospect list on the recommendation of a current donor.

Look for attendees who benefit from benefits

Second, answer the question, "Who could benefit from an event experience?" Organizations with a mission of importance to women and young professionals are finding that, from a potential donor's perspective, buying an event ticket is a prerequisite to making an annual gift. An extensive donor research and marketing report conducted on behalf of the Women's Funding Network (Hathaway, 1998) found that women donors and prospective donors valued special events sponsored by nonprofits because of the opportunity to be with like-minded women. This audience values relationships and, for them, benefits are an occasion to develop or build on alliances. For many women, event attendance opens the gateway to unrestricted gifts. Similarly, a priority for baby boomers (people born between 1946 and 1964) is building a large system of extended family, friends, and colleagues. Events are an opportunity for boomers to create, find, and nurture affiliations. These two audiences value the service of relationship-building and value the organization providing the service. This is an excellent stage from which to build a donor relationship.

Educating event attendees

Education is important in any development effort. For-profit marketers frequently chant, "Tell, tell, tell before you sell." In the donor conversion process, education is critical to overcome two common problems.

Find the educational opportunities

First, benefit attendees often leave an event knowing more about the event and its corporate sponsors than about the nonprofit host. Creating a connection to your organization—not to the event—should be the goal. How many "teachable moments" is your organization failing to profit from or (worse) giving away?

In printed materials and from the podium we hail the volunteer organizers and herald financial support. Signage at some charity events rivals that found at professional sporting events. Take these opportunities back, and use them to educate buyers about your organization and its work.

From the podium. Your audience is most in tune during the first few minutes of the program. Instead of devoting that time to a laundry list of thank you's, start with information about the mission and successes of the organization. Prepare the buyer for future contact by sharing key points from the case statement that will be used in an annual appeal. Keep it short and keep the attention on the reason for being there.

On signage. If signage is part of the event, be sure your organization is represented. Invest in a professional sign and keep the size of sponsor signs at or below the size of your own. Look for opportunities to share tidbits of information through signage. Table tents, hole signs, or auction table plaques can impart information about the number of clients served or the products offered. Find a unique way at your event to inform without overwhelming.

In printed materials. When a printed program is appropriate, designate space to tell your story. This can be accomplished through a narrative statement, a testimonial from a client, or an advertisement describing a service or product your organization offers.

Use information as education

The second common problem is that eventgoers confuse buying with donating. The rhetoric of ticket-selling reinforces this confusion. Materials describe the tax-deductible portion of the gift and encourage ticket sales as a way to "support the work of XYZ charity." This language first found a home in the traditional annual appeal solicitations. Clarify the buyer's understanding of the difference through information. An event is one avenue for disseminating this information.

As the preceding paragraphs suggest, the event program becomes a vehicle for informing attendees about the bigger picture. Clearly state how proceeds from the event are used and how proceeds from the annual fund drive are used. Printed programs can bolster the message by announcing when an annual drive begins and its purpose. The clarification process is reinforced in postevent materials (described in the following section).

Successfully shifting attention to—or back to—the organization and its mission does require advance work with volunteers. Committee members who have worked on other events expect that the practice of top-of-the-program recognition will continue. Members soliciting corporate sponsorship are accustomed to promising the farm and the most prominent sign placement at the event. Educate your volunteers about the goal and the process. Most volunteers are committed to the organization and can understand that the event is not the goal but rather a medium for building support.

Cultivating event attendees

Many analyses on the effectiveness of special events as cultivation opportunities conclude, "Benefits don't raise $1 million gifts." Few chance encounters do. Rather, the development process shows that large gifts have been the result of nurturing over a period of time, and they reflect the donor's growing link to the organization and the donor's growing involvement (Rosso, 1991, p. 53). Planning to cultivate turns the traditional event environment of chance encounter into an opportunity to develop links.

Make connections

The key to developing the opportunity is getting your leaders and key volunteers to events and getting them out from behind the check-in table. Before each event, compare the attendance list with your prospect lists. Let solicitors know who will be there and assign them one to three individuals (depending on the length and format of the benefit) to "connect with." Your team should be coached on the goals of the not-so-chance encounter. Although usually not appropriate for soliciting (or as a substitute for soliciting), events are excellent for informal dialoguing. By delving into the interests and concerns of the attendees and assessing their understanding of the organization, your team can gain valuable background. Although we have many opportunities to *talk to* our potential customers (newsletters, solicitations, invitations, advertisements), we have few opportunities to *hear from them* (Peppers and Rogers, 1993, p. 209). An event can provide an occasion for listening. Furnish solicitors with feedback forms to complete after the event, and update the prospect file with information and impressions gained during the meeting.

Gain experience

Events can also provide a forum for your volunteers to become more comfortable with soliciting and gain experience. These kinds of informal encounters serve to create a sense of comfort and familiarity between solicitor and potential donor.

Again, it requires advance work with volunteers to use events as a place for cultivation. The preparation should help them understand that this type of cultivation is not a substitute for one-on-one solicitation. Briefing volunteers on the entire development effort and their role in the process is an essential step in any successful development plan. It is especially important in a conversion program. Working individually with some of the attendees is part of later solicitations.

Soliciting event attendees

"Why don't our gala guests respond to our year-end letters?" This question is as certain to be asked as chicken is to be served. Before delving into the solicitation-to-conversion process, it is important to recognize the "givens."

Given 1. Not everyone who is solicited to support an organization gives a gift. Most annual campaigns use a gift range chart that anticipates that 25 percent to 50 percent of prospects will make a gift at the level requested. Expecting all buyers to become donors is not realistic.

Given 2. Not every special event attendee is a potential donor. As discussed earlier, the key is determining where the possible overlap is and focusing efforts on those individuals.

Given 3. Targeted segments respond to targeted messages. It is unrealistic to expect that benefit attendees will respond to the same appeal that draws previous donors.

Given 4. Being asked to give a gift usually precedes giving a gift. Ticket buyers will not become donors if they are not solicited.

Each of the givens is self-evident. Yet many fundraisers fail to acknowledge these truths and consequently dismiss the ability of special events to be useful beyond the fun and funds that they raise. These truisms serve as a framework for the solicitation of ticket buyers.

Set goals and expectations

What would you (or your board) expect with an annual campaign goal as vague as "raising some money?" Most organizations achieve the best results with measurable *action goals:* raise $300,000; increase the number of donors by 10 percent; upgrade one hundred donors. Goals require planning, setting reasonable expectations, and properly assigning resources. Some thought should be given to a conversion goal before the event, and the best prospects should have had contact with members of your solicitation team. If not, this is the time to set an action goal (or revise it based on feedback from event contacts with prospects). Start your thinking at 10 percent (for every one hundred attendees, ten make a gift). The goal is converting buyers into donors. The objective is converting 10 percent of the buyers.

Some behaviors indicate higher potential for giving and for conversion:

- Multiple ticket buying (over a number of years or with a number of events)

- Solid contact meetings (at the events or in other settings)
- Attendance at mission-specific events (buyers are demonstrating like-mindedness), and
- Preparation for solicitation (buyers are educated about the organization and informed of differing types of support)

The goal might also be set higher if an organization has a track record of converting buyers. A good rule of thumb is an additional 3 percent for every evident buyer behavior and an additional 5 percent for track record.

If your organization holds multiple events, set conversion goals for buyers at each event. Treating each event independently also allows an organization to compare results with techniques used at each event and to improve the model for conversion on an ongoing basis.

Determine the message

It is not uncommon for an organization to select event attendees for solicitation by direct mail and then send the same letter to every donor and prospect at the lower end of the annual fund gift chart. Yet ticket-buying nondonors are not at the same place in their relationship with the organization as previous donors. Asking them to "continue to support" your good work is not the most effective approach for them. In fact, it will erode any success made in clarifying the difference between buying and donating—if you communicate with them as donors, they are likely to think of themselves as donors. Meet these prospects where they are in the relationship.

If, as suggested, events are considered a part of the entire development plan and if a prospective pool of attendees has been included in the cultivation process, then some attendees will be included in the personal-visits portion of your solicitation plan. Others may be more appropriate for a targeted approach by mail.

When going one-on-one

Don't be discouraged by small numbers in the attendees-prospects-personal solicitation chain. In many ways, a smaller number indicates an effective process. Qualifying necessarily eliminates names at each step and, for all practical purposes, most organizations couldn't begin to solicit every attendee personally.

The process of personal visits, by a team or an individual, has been well-documented, but some specific suggestions relevant to visits with event attendees will be helpful. First, acknowledge their participation with an event or events in the initial remarks. Be deliberate and specific in the language used. If you say, "We appreciate your support," that suggests to them that they are donors. If that phrase is used it should be followed with the name of the event supported. A more precise statement would be, "We appreciate your involvement in our annual golf outing." Second, frame the conversation in the context of what *other* ways they can be involved in the organization—most significantly, as a donor. Using specific language and concentrating on different ways to be connected also preempts the typical "I'm already a supporter" response from ticket buyers during their first personal visit. The idea is to distinguish the difference without diminishing the value of their involvement. Finally, be prepared to discuss the differences between event participation and donations. A natural by-product of educating prospects and making distinctions in financial involvement is more informed prospects and more informed questions. Brief everyone involved in the visit about benefits' purpose, costs, and proceeds allocation.

When soliciting by mail

Like special events, some mail solicitation is a necessity. Ticket buyers who have not been involved in any cultivation activities are candidates for a targeted letter. The emphasis here is on *targeted*. You can accomplish this by incorporating into your letter the suggestions offered earlier. Acknowledge participation, invite other involvement, and educate prospects about the differences. The return on letters will improve if the signature or note is from someone to whom the receiver is likely to respond. Follow-up phone calls add to the success.

A request by mail should occur within thirty days of an event. This is the window during which you can take advantage of the event education and cultivation activities. The key to any successful fundraising program is what occurs after your initial contact (Nichols, 1995, p. 67). If you can't turn a request out in thirty days, be sure that the next piece of mail a prospect receives is something other than an invitation to another event. Only inviting that person to benefits implies that this is the only value you see in the relationship. It sends the message that you think of that person as a ticket buyer. Asking for a contribution lets the buyer know that he or she can also be a donor.

Evaluating the conversion plan

If the first mantra of for-profit marketers is, "Tell, tell, tell before you sell," the second is, "Test, test, test before you rest." It is unlikely that you will be happy with your first buyer-to-donor conversion plan. Initially, it will be difficult to break the mold of event planning and evaluation. There are several questions to ask in evaluating your plan:

- Is there an understanding—among staff, key volunteers, and donors—about the difference between a buyer and donor?
- Are we including education about the *core* work of our organization in all event literature and programs?
- Have we analyzed our donor base to determine who is a donor, who is an event attendee, and who is both?
- Have we seriously reviewed even a handful of eventgoers for their ability to be donors?
- How have we improved the solicitation of nonevent gifts from ticket buyers (starting to solicit, having a targeted solicitation, including prospective donors from the event pool in personal visits)?
- What improvements will be made on the conversion plan for the next event or the next year's event?

The initial evaluation questions do not ask how many buyers you were able to convert. Is this important? Will you receive a cold meal at the next benefit luncheon you plan or attend? *Yes!* However, it is also important to evaluate the plan based on the new information you have gathered about prospects, the new level of awareness in your organization, and the improvements associated with integrating events in the total development plan as a cultivation opportunity. As for numbers, as noted earlier, don't set you sights much above a 30 percent conversion rate.

How long to wait

Most database marketers have a two-year rule of thumb. If you have no response from a prospect (she doesn't attend, call for more information, make a gift, and so on) after twenty-four months, it is time to reconsider that person's status as a prospect. If you do not see improving linkages (annual fund gift, volunteer activity, and so on) two years after attendance at an event, it is time to reevaluate her status. Reassess each potential donor on an individual basis. Eventually, you will face the question, "Should we consider dropping someone who faithfully attends our $25 luncheon?" There are as many answers as there are organizations asking the question. Consider the year-round resources spent for the $25 ticket buyer (which may only yield $10 after expenses). Consider asking the attendee if she is interested in any activity beyond the lunch. Consider trying a more aggressive conversion tactic (see the following paragraph), especially if this is a prospect that has been qualified through a variety of means. Consider making her record "inactive" and devoting your resources to converting another buyer.

What if you're not ready to give up?

If you want to try one more test before classifying someone as a perpetual ticket buyer, think about sending a tribute or memorial request to that persistent event attendee. Many individuals will consider giving in honor of or in the name of someone else before they are ready to give an unrestricted gift in their own name. This request can be done simply and inexpensively through the mail. You will have greater success with a tribute or memorial solicitation if it is received around a traditional holiday (Mother's Day,

Valentine's Day, Thanksgiving). If this is not possible, be sure to give recipients a laundry list of occasions for giving a gift in honor of someone (birthday, graduation, new job, anniversary, birth of a child or grandchild, and so on). Some may consider this a special event by mail. Finally, don't dismiss the potential of a donor who gives an unrestricted gift through a tribute or memorial. Although the conversion rate of ticket buyer to memorial donor may be low, many organizations find the conversion of memorial donor to annual fund donor to be very high.

Conclusion

Few first-time conversion plans can be fully implemented. Knowing what it takes to make a successful plan may cause your organization to delay the attempt even longer. If your organization cannot mount the full plan, try any one piece of it as soon as your next event. Make that first step manageable and easy to appraise. Give one name each to three of your key volunteers and ask each to connect with that attendee. Encourage the volunteer to share one key message about your organization and to ask the attendee how he learned about the event and what he knows about the work you do in the community. Collect the results and be sure to update the attendee's record with the new information. Have the volunteer send a personal note thanking the attendee for participating in the event. Be sure to ask the attendee for a gift before the impact of the personal touch expires. Adjust your next plan based on the outcome of your test.

All nonprofits need to earn and maintain the highest level of confidence and support from their community (donors and nondonors alike). How money is raised and managed is a key factor in the public's determination of that organization's value (Billitteri and Blum, 1998). Because events have evolved into stand-alone activities, their value and the public's perception of the host organization's value are being challenged. Although most of us are not in a position to eliminate events, we can ensure that they do not become a great personal, financial, and organizational resource abyss. With a plan to integrate events into the total development process, an event can be an effective tool for introducing prospects to an organization and setting them on the path toward becoming donors.

It is difficult to imagine an event that isn't staff-intensive or doesn't burn out volunteers. But an event that generates new donors can be more than a figment of our imagination.

References

Billitteri, T. J., and Blum, D. E. "Unsettled Accounts." *Chronicle of Philanthropy*, Mar. 26, 1998, pp. 41–51.

Goodman, B. " Nonprofits Are in an Uproar over 98-2." *Nonprofit Times*, Apr. 1998, pp. 31–32.

Hathaway, B. *Women's Funding Network Donor Research and Marketing Report.* Denver: Ordinary Magic, 1998.

Miller, M. P. "Nine and a Half Theses About Fundraising Benefits: Rationalizations, Indulgences, and Opportunity Costs." In D. F. Burlingame and W. F. Ilchman (eds.), *Alternative Revenue Sources.* New Directions for Philanthropic Fundraising, no. 12. San Francisco: Jossey-Bass, 1996.

Nichols, J. E. *Growing from Good to Great.* Chicago: Bonus Books, 1995.

Peppers, D., and Rogers, M. *The One-to-One Future.* New York: Doubleday, 1993.

Rosso, H. A. "The Annual Fund: A Building Block for Fund Raising." In H. A. Rosso and Associates, *Achieving Excellence in Fund Raising: A Comprehensive Guide to Principles, Strategies, and Methods.* San Francisco: Jossey-Bass, 1991.

TRACY WAYSON *is the director of the Women's Fund of the Milwaukee Foundation and consults with not-for-profit organizations on a variety of development issues.*

Small nonprofits have important strengths for fundraising. But they also face many critical obstacles. Organizational leaders, technical assistance providers, consultants, trainers, and grant makers and other major donors need to make realistic assessments of small nonprofits' fundraising strengths and weaknesses and provide assistance accordingly.

7

Small is beautiful—but is it always viable?

Michael Page Miller

MOST NONPROFITS are small. Most major nonprofits today started as small operations. Numerous innovative programs and solutions to major problems facing this country have originated with small nonprofits. Many Americans' primary volunteer experience is with a small, local organization, including neighborhood groups and churches.

Yet the fundraising profession, college and university nonprofit management courses, and academic classes in the burgeoning field of philanthropic studies pay scant attention to fundraising in smaller nonprofits. This is particularly unfortunate because the most significant challenge facing smaller nonprofits concerns developing effective, ongoing fundraising programs. Technical assistance providers, consultants, trainers, and grant makers and other major

NEW DIRECTIONS FOR PHILANTHROPIC FUNDRAISING, NO. 20, SUMMER 1998 © JOSSEY-BASS PUBLISHERS

donors dedicated to supporting small nonprofits need to understand their strengths and even more importantly their weaknesses when it comes to effective fundraising.

Seven elements are important to a strong fundraising program for all organizations, small and large. These are the elements:

- A well-articulated case for support
- Identifiable donor constituencies
- Diversity of support, both in gift sizes and markets, with a strong commitment to developing an individual donor base
- Leaders who champion fundraising
- A functioning board that is involved in setting the organization's direction
- Board participation in giving and fundraising
- Sufficient organizational resources devoted to fundraising, such as staff, systems, and budget

Each of these elements can present special obstacles for small organizations.

Small nonprofits' fundraising strengths

It is important to note the fundraising strengths of small nonprofits. These strengths can be potent magnets for attracting donors and can form the foundation for dealing with fundraising obstacles.

Mission-driven nature. The key players in many small nonprofits are often motivated by strong political, philosophical, moral, ethical, or religious beliefs. This is particularly true of grassroots and advocacy organizations. On an organizational level, these values are manifest in a well-defined mission. The mission reflects the shared values or philosophy of the key players in the organization (Rosso and Associates, 1991, p. 40).

Dedication to fundamental change. Many small community-based groups and advocacy organizations are dedicated to creating fundamental changes in the social, political, economic, or religious structures of society.

Innovative and entrepreneurial nature. Large, well-established organizations are like a "powerful locomotive . . . everything functioning predictably, energy being efficiently transformed into forward motion, but no learning, no innovation, no possibility of going anywhere except where the tracks lead" (Gardner, 1988, p. 4). By contrast, small nonprofits can offer donors innovation, flexibility, and an entrepreneurial spirit.

Closeness to the problem. Many small nonprofits were founded or are led by individuals who are directly affected by the issue they are attacking—for example, tenants who organize to challenge a slumlord. This closeness to the problem can lead to new insights and innovative solutions that might be missed by larger, more established organizations whose leaders have lost touch with the grass roots.

Efficiency. With low overhead, low payroll, and high reliance on volunteers, small nonprofits can stretch donated dollars very far.

Strong organizing skills. Effective fundraising is a process, and the process must be organized and managed. Leaders and staff in community-based organizations, for example, often have very strong campaign organizing skills. (The strong parallels between community organizing and fundraising are discussed in a later section.)

Small nonprofits' fundraising weaknesses: When size is an issue

Few of the obstacles to effective fundraising are limited to small nonprofits. Many items identified here can be found in a nonprofit institution of any size. However, small nonprofits are more likely to have a concentration of these challenges and fewer flexible resources for dealing with them. Most critically, the strategies for addressing the fundraising obstacles in small nonprofits are often significantly different from those used in larger organizations.

Smallness itself brings with it a group of practical problems that can undermine efforts to develop or expand an organization's fundraising program.

Lack of staff resources

Many small nonprofits lack the paid or volunteer staff resources to organize and support a fundraising program. Often, staff members are stretched too thin by the demands of their program and other administrative duties. The time and energy they do have for fundraising may be devoted to securing the one or two grants that can underwrite the organization completely.

The problem is compounded when neither the staff nor board leadership recognizes that staff support and leadership are critical to fundraising. As a priority, fundraising is often a far distant second to program implementation. And time devoted to developing fundraising skills and knowledge is often considered a luxury.

One important reason why board members and other volunteers fail to become effectively engaged in fundraising is lack of staff support. Volunteers are most effective when they receive training, coaching, encouragement, and information and materials, and when they can operate in a structured environment. This is particularly true when it comes to fundraising. Sending a volunteer off with ten names to solicit without any support is a classic recipe for failure.

Small leadership cadre

Small organizations often have small leadership cadres. Hence there are fewer opportunities to find the one or two individuals who might champion a new fundraising culture in the organization. Conversely, an organization in which there is an infusion of new executive staff or new board members is often in the best position to change fundraising attitudes and practices.

Single-funder syndrome

Nonprofits are often launched by a single foundation grant or a gift from an individual "angel." The longer an organization is wholly or largely dependent on this single funder and the longer the board and staff are allowed to ignore the need to develop a diverse fundraising program, the more that dependency grows. When the single funder moves on after providing a three- or four-year seed grant, the need to change both attitudes and behavior is great but extremely difficult to make happen. The first reaction may be to try to look for another one or two gift solutions rather than to develop a broader constituency for support.

Lack of experience with successful models and attitudes

The board and staff members of smaller, community-based organizations often lack fundraising experience, or more important, they lack experience with the fundraising models and principles that underlie the most successful practices.

Overreliance on events

The fundraising strategy most common among individuals involved in small nonprofits is event-related: dinners, various "-athons," sale of tickets or raffle chances, and pursuit of underwriters. The key word here is *selling*. Members of an organization who sell tickets to a benefit dance believe that they are giving something back to the buyer, rather than soliciting an outright gift to the organization.

Founder's influence

Many small nonprofits survive for years on the dedication of one or two individuals. Often these are the organization's founders or very early leaders, or these dedicated individuals have been involved for so long that they have reinvented the organization to fit their own personalities.

If the founder is still the leader and exhibits classic "founder's syndrome"—with all power concentrated in one individual—then progress is rarely possible. Even when the founder is not the formal leader but is still involved as a key player, then that person's experiences and attitudes with fundraising will color everyone else's. For example, if the founder does not believe that the board should take on meaningful fundraising activities then it is highly unlikely the board members will move past that. Either the founder will have to change his or her behavior (unlikely) or new leaders will have to evolve who are willing to ignore or work around the founder (very difficult).

Founding board influence and lack of board turnover

Closely related to the founder's syndrome problem is the issue of a founding board. The operational norms that a new board develops are shaped by the board members' early experiences. When fundraising expectations are not part of the culture and when the board is dominated by founders or longtime members, then it will be very difficult to create a fundraising culture.

Whenever there is a lack of turnover or regular infusion of new members into the board, norms and behaviors are very likely to become rigid. Unless there is a severe crisis, changing the board's norms will be difficult.

Small nonprofits' fundraising weaknesses: "Not us" issues

Another set of obstacles to fundraising found in small nonprofits are attitudes and beliefs that could be termed *not us* issues.

An aversion to marketing. Successful fundraising is based on appealing to the values or needs of a donor. This requires a marketing orientation, that is, an understanding that donors give because they receive something back. Leaders of small nonprofits may lack experience or have an aversion to marketing. These individuals may see marketing as a compromise of their values. They may impose a values test on donors: "Only other true believers can understand what we do, so we will only talk to other true believers." Nichols (1996) explores an aversion to marketing among what she terms "passionate" organizations: "Passionate organizations often display characteristics which can create barriers to their ability to communicate effectively outside 'the family'. . . . [There is a] conscious separating out from the rest of the world. The vision is lived out on a daily basis. Sometimes, deliberately or not, this results in a 'they versus we' posturing. Communication with those not part of the inner circle is strained."

"Poor people are not generous." In spite of daily examples around them, many individuals with low or moderate incomes do not believe that they and their neighbors are generous or can provide meaningful financial support to any organization. Organizers who work in poor communities often share this belief.

"Our people are not generous." This is a variation on the "poor people are not generous" theme. For example, the leaders of Puerto Rican organizations will believe that Puerto Ricans are not generous. The variations are many—women, public interest lawyers, teachers, social workers, artists, residents of Maine, Italian Americans, people in rural communities—they either cannot afford to give, cannot give meaningful amounts, or lack a tradition of giving. In short, the feeling is, "We can avoid fundraising among those we serve and involve because they cannot or will not give."

"We don't know anyone with money." This statement most likely means, "We are not comfortable asking for gifts from people we know," or "The amounts we would get from the people we know are too small to matter."

"We will corrupt the board." Lacking personal experience with philanthropic individuals, the leaders of grassroots and community organizations have great difficulty believing that their board members could give a personally significant gift (Rosso and Associates, 1991, p. 138), help with fundraising, and remain dedicated to the organization's mission. "If we make fundraising a board role, we will lose good board members we already have and need, we will be forced to bring on people who will corrupt or compromise our mission, or both," is how this thought goes.

Strategies for assisting small nonprofits

The issues and attitudes outlined in the previous paragraphs can present significant—in some cases, insurmountable—obstacles to developing effective fundraising programs in small nonprofit organizations. Trainers, technical assistance providers, consultants, and funders of community-based organizations cannot afford to ignore these obstacles in designing and delivering programs dedicated to helping small nonprofits.

The following paragraphs suggest some strategies for delivering more effective assistance to small nonprofits.

Perform a triage

Focus help where it will be most effective. Most individuals dedicated to helping smaller nonprofits want to believe that every organization with a good mission and a real constituency can and should succeed. Unfortunately, this is not realistic. Small may be beautiful, but it is not always viable. It may be necessary to perform a triage when evaluating small nonprofits so that efforts can be concentrated where they would be useful. Hence, organizations needing fundraising help could be divided into three groups:

Those capable of succeeding largely on their own. Key elements are largely in place. These organizations have the right culture, leadership, and essential resources to develop effective fundraising programs. For these groups, training, fundraising audits, and some ongoing consulting will often be sufficient. Other strategies that would be effective include creating a fundraising support network and networking for staff.

Those that have significant obstacles to success but also have leaders willing to take on those obstacles. This group should receive most of the resources, including training, fundraising audits, and ongoing consulting support.

Those that have significant obstacles but lack leadership dedicated to change. Investing in building fundraising capacity will be ineffective.

Recognize the limits of training

Training workshops and presentations are among the most common forms of technical assistance provided to small nonprofit organizations. This is not surprising because, compared with other types of assistance, training is usually less expensive and requires less of a time commitment by the participants. In short, "training is a low wattage intervention" (Jones, 1996, p. 411). But once the training session ends, participants often have little motivation or support "back home" to adopt and maintain new behaviors.

Still, as with any intervention, training alone is most effective with participants who already have the right orientation toward fundraising but lack some direction and technical skills (the first group in the triage). For those most in need of help, training alone seldom makes a significant difference. These organizations need ongoing support.

Trainers and training organizations could make a significant difference by redefining their own role so that they also function as organizational consultants and engage in ongoing collaborations with clients to change an organization's culture (Jones, 1996, p. 411).

Move out of the comfort zone

Leaders in most nonprofits pick consultants and technical assistance providers with whom they are comfortable. This comfortable feeling often also means that the basic assumptions in the organizational culture sustaining major fundraising obstacles are not challenged. Although compatibility is important, it is also important that consultants to small nonprofits help these organizations stretch and take on expanded fundraising challenges, such as developing the board and tapping new constituencies.

Practice what you teach

Consultants and other technical assistance providers teach what they know. In many cities, the local grant-making community provides support for nonprofit technical assistance organizations whose focus is largely smaller nonprofits. Many of these technical assistance organizations are themselves primarily, if not entirely, grant supported. These organizations must be challenged to expand their own fundraising programs so they can teach and effectively model new behaviors for their clients.

Develop a national, small nonprofit support network

Small nonprofits need their own national fundraising support group with local chapters. Such a group does not exist today. Most individuals involved in fundraising for small organizations have never heard of the National Society of Fund Raising Executives. The support networks that do exist for small nonprofits, grassroots, and advocacy organizations are organized around specific areas of work, such as housing and community development, educational advocacy, or the environment. Fundraising is usually only a small part of the network agenda and too often the assistance offered is limited to grant-writing workshops.

Success stories and models

Individuals and organizations dedicated to helping small nonprofits also need both examples of success and models to help understand small nonprofit organizational development.

Documented examples of success

There are certainly examples of smaller, grassroots organizations developing effective fundraising programs involving their boards and tapping into a diverse constituency. However, they are not well documented. Or if they are well documented, they are not well known. The best documentation currently exists in the *Grassroots Fundraising Journal* (Klein, all issues). Trainers and other providers need more and better documented case studies. Individual leaders and staff members from successful small organizations should be available to bear witness to their peers.

Organizational development models that fit small nonprofits

Current models used to track and analyze nonprofit organizational development have limited utility when it comes to small nonprofits. The primary problem is that they assume a level of resources that is not realistic for small organizations. There need to be new models that track the development of healthy small nonprofits and their fundraising programs.

Community organizing as a model

One organizational development model that should be explored for its usefulness to small nonprofit fundraising is traditional community organizing, based on the theories and practices of Saul Alinsky (Alinsky, 1989, 1991). Community organizing practices and theory have evolved significantly since Alinsky, and several different schools of organizing have developed. There are many common fundamental elements and these elements are directly applicable to developing fundraising capacity in small organizations.

Community organizing is about empowering community residents to articulate their own needs, develop their solutions, and undertake actions to achieve these solutions. Fundraising empowers all: the donor, the individual who solicits gifts, and the organization as a whole. The more members of the organization involved in fundraising and the more diverse the sources of support, the more powerful the organization.

Other community organizing elements that translate into good fundraising include these:

Working with indigenous leaders. Fundraising requires strong volunteer leadership, ideally those individuals who already have the respect of their neighbors and colleagues and who will set an example by their own willingness to give and get.

Talking to people in the community to identify their issues and concerns. Asking questions and listening is a key strategy for cultivating and soliciting donors. It is the opposite of selling.

Building on intermediate victories or small winnable issues. Fundraising works best when it is conceived and organized in campaign terms. Every gift solicited is a "victory." (These victories may come in very short time periods rather than taking the years that winning issues often require.) Smaller fundraising campaigns will lead to larger ones.

Appealing to self-interest. This is fundamental to marketing. The most
effective fundraisers always appeal to the donor's self-interest—
but not necessarily to selfish interests.

Accountability to the community. Organizations that seek funds from
their own community must be accountable to succeed.

How grant makers can help

Grant makers are often the largest funders of the small nonprofit
organizations they support. As such, grant makers need to consider
how to use their leverage to encourage the development of more
effective fundraising programs. Unfortunately, many are reluctant
to "interfere" with the internal operations of their grantee organizations. They may provide funding for technical assistance and
training, help open doors, and be generous with their advice but
will not impose requirements.

However, grant makers and other major funders should reex-
amine their approaches if they want to ensure that their grantees
are still in business after their grant support has ended. Examples
of leverage that grant makers should consider when making or
renewing grants include these:

Require that grantees establish guidelines for boards, such as a 100
   percent giving policy among board members (which can be
   accomplished by asking for "personally significant gifts"); the
   inclusion of fundraising as a board member responsibility; a
   board rotation policy to ensure fresh attitudes and enthusiasm;
   and board involvement in strategic planning to help promote
   real ownership of the program.

Require that there be an individual who will provide a specific min-
   imum percentage of time to fundraising.

Provide grants for organizational development instead of or in
   addition to program grants.

Offer challenge grants for organizations to solicit broader support,
   especially from individuals. The Kresge Foundation through its
   challenges has been remarkably effective in encouraging well-

planned and well-executed capital campaigns that serve an organization for years after the close of the campaign.

Set standards for diversity of funding sources in the second and third years.

Reevaluate the impact of training alone; offer more extensive consulting assistance.

Help recruit board members.

Grant makers who are not already doing so can help small nonprofits by making introductions to other donors and providing exposure to their local grant-making community.

Fundraising federations

Another strategy that both small nonprofits and grant makers should consider is developing fundraising federations for small nonprofits. Federated fundraising directly addresses the issue of smallness itself. There are already successful examples of federated fundraising for small nonprofits in several cities, most notably among women's organizations.

Grant makers can underwrite the development of the federation or provide challenge grants to encourage federated fundraising. A federation can solicit grants, encourage workplace campaigns, and more. To be successful, however, a federation must be more than a mere collaboration. A federation must have its own staff and a board with a majority of members not representing federation member organizations. A federation can also engage staff or consultants to work with member organizations on board development and fundraising from individuals.

Conclusion

It is easy to romanticize small nonprofits: they provide a rich and diverse tapestry of civic involvement in this country, are a critical source of innovative ideas and solutions to major social issues, represent the true voice of the people, and so on. However, these visions will be significantly strengthened if small nonprofits begin to receive the same level of study, analysis, and organizational development support that mainstream nonprofits currently receive. Those individuals and institutions already engaged in nurturing small nonprofits have a special responsibility to recognize that current support programs may be inadequate and sometimes mistargeted and to develop and sustain new approaches.

References

Alinsky, S. D. *Rules for Radicals*. New York: Vintage Books, 1989.

Alinsky, S. D. *Reveille for Radicals*. New York: Vintage Books, 1991.

Gardner, J. W. *Renewing: The Leader's Creative Task*. Washington, D.C.: INDE-PENDENT SECTOR, 1988.

Jones, J. E. "Training as a Strategic Intervention." In J. E. Jones, W. L. Bearley, and D. C. Watsabaugh (eds.), *The New Fieldbook for Trainers: Tips, Tools, and Techniques*. Amherst, Mass.: HRD Press, 1996.

Klein, K. (ed.). *Grassroots Fundraising Journal*. Berkeley, Calif.: Chardon Press (all issues).

Nichols, J. E. "A Move to 'Passionate' Organizations." *Contributions*, Jan. 1996, pp. 411–412.

Rosso, H. A., and Associates. *Achieving Excellence in Fund Raising: A Comprehensive Guide to Principles, Strategies, and Methods*. San Francisco: Jossey-Bass, 1991.

MICHAEL PAGE MILLER *is a founder of Miller/Rollins, a fundraising and management consulting firm in Putnam Valley, New York, and a lead faculty member at The Fund Raising School.*

Index

Back Issue/Subscription Order Form

Copy or detach and send to:
Jossey-Bass Inc., Publishers, 350 Sansome Street, San Francisco CA 94104-1342

Call or fax toll free!
Phone 888-378-2537 6AM–5PM PST; Fax 800-605-2665

Back issues: Please send me the following issues at $25 each
(Important: please include series initials and issue number, such as PF90)

1. PF _____

_____

_____

$ _____ Total for single issues

$ _____ Shipping charges (for single issues **only;** subscriptions are exempt
from shipping charges): Up to $30, add $5^{50} • $30^{01}–$50, add $6^{50}
$50^{01}–$75, add $7^{50} • $75^{01}–$100, add $9 • $100^{01}–$150, add $10
Over $150, call for shipping charge

Subscriptions   Please ❏ start   ❏ renew my subscription to *New Directions
for Philanthropic Fundraising* for the year 19___ at the following
rate:

      ❏ Individual $67   ❏ Institutional $115
NOTE: Subscriptions are quarterly, and are for the calendar year only.
Subscriptions begin with the spring issue of the year indicated above.
For shipping outside the U.S., please add $25.

$ _____ Total single issues and subscriptions (CA, IN, NJ, NY and DC
residents, add sales tax for single issues. NY and DC residents must
include shipping charges when calculating sales tax. NY and Canadian
residents only, add sales tax for subscriptions)

❏ Payment enclosed (U.S. check or money order only)

❏ VISA, MC, AmEx, Discover Card #_____ Exp. date_____

Signature _____ Day phone _____

❏ Bill me (U.S. institutional orders only. Purchase order required)

Purchase order #_____

Name _____

Address _____

_____

_____

Phone_____ E-mail _____

For more information about Jossey-Bass Publishers, visit our Web site at:
www.josseybass.com   **PRIORITY CODE = ND1**

Previous Issues Available

PF4 Achieving Trustee Involvement in Fundraising, *Timothy L. Seiler, Kay Sprinkel Grace*

PF3 Financial Practices for Effective Fundraising, *James M. Greenfield*

PF2 Women as Donors, Women as Philanthropists, *Abbie J. von Schlegell, Joan M. Fisher*

PF1 Fundraising Matters: True Stories of How Raising Funds Fulfills Dreams, *Michael Seltzer*